Umberto's Kitchen

Umberto's Kitchen

THE FLAVOURS OF TUSCANY

Umberto Menghi

Douglas & McIntyre

Vancouver/Toronto

First paperback printing 1997

01 5 4

Douglas & McIntyre
2323 Quebec Street, Suite 201
Vancouver, British Columbia
V5T 4S7

Canadian Cataloguing in Publication Data
Menghi, Umberto, 1946–
    Umberto's Kitchen
    Includes index.
    ISBN 1-55054-506-X
    1. Cookery, Italian—Tuscan style. 2. Cookery, Canadian. I. Title
TX723.2.T86M45 1995   641.5945'5   C95-910345-7

Cover photo by John Sherlock Studio Ltd.
Cover and book design by DesignGeist
Printed and bound in Hong Kong by C & C Offset Printing Co. Ltd.
Printed on acid-free paper ∞

The publisher gratefully acknowledges the assistance of the Canada Council for the arts and of the
British Columbia Ministry of Tourism, Small Business and Culture for its publishing programs.

*The publisher would like to thank Del Miller and Nick Ringma at Casa, 420 Howe Street,
Vancouver for the dinnerware, glassware and cutlery used in the food photographs. Ceramic tiles
were supplied by World Mosaic, 1665 West 7th Avenue, Vancouver.*

Acknowledgements

Not only has writing this book made me remember the good times I have had with food, the pleasure of entertaining people and the lively lifestyle of the restaurant business, it has also brought to mind all the people I have been associated with who have been so much a part of my growing up and my business success. I don't think my publisher has allowed enough pages for me to recall every one of them, but I must mention a few.

First, I must thank my mother, Delia, for teaching me love and respect for food from an early age. Second, although I didn't always appreciate it at the time, thanks go to my father for his strong discipline while I was growing up. *Respect* is the word that comes to mind whenever I have to make a decision now, and I can sincerely say that without the early support of my family, and the strength they passed on to me, I probably wouldn't be here talking about it.

Family includes my sister Marietta Malacarne, who is happiest when preparing food. I have never seen her working in the kitchen without a smile, and how her face lights up with joy when people around her table ask for seconds. Only after everyone is served will she join others at the meal. In that respect, she is a reflection of Mamma Delia. Marietta's husband, Silvano, is general manager of the Tuscany estate and Villa Delia. My older sister, Guiliana Pratelli, is ever ready to organize a special event or to assist in creating one and can always be counted on, with her husband, Alessandro, to arrange an occasion with ease and elegance.

As for my brother, Andriano—the professor—he was always the most punctual at mealtime (even as a youth, he demanded that meals start on time). It is critically important for him that everyone sit down together and partake of the food, for food stimulates conversation; then he can talk and argue and interact with everyone.

The rest of my family, all my relatives, gave me energy and educated me with their togetherness—over food and wine. They showed me the importance of approaching the table with the right attitude and encouraged me to willingly share my sentiments and feelings in a congenial atmosphere.

Now that I am constantly working in my restaurants with more than 500 staff members, I am most closely in touch with my chefs, particularly il maestro Gianni Picchi—artist, sculptor, philosopher, poet—who every day expresses himself in a different way, but always artistically. He is forever ready to please and always ready for a little argument if things are not quite right for him. Not only is being around these creative people a challenge—all my days are challenges—but watching and absorbing their ways of going about their work stimulates my sense of professionalism.

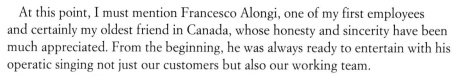

At this point, I must mention Francesco Alongi, one of my first employees and certainly my oldest friend in Canada, whose honesty and sincerity have been much appreciated. From the beginning, he was always ready to entertain with his operatic singing not just our customers but also our working team.

Runaway chef Ron Lammie (back and forth from one job to another), another old-time friend and innovative cook, is a refreshing, energetic person who could always stimulate my taste buds with his culinary creations, but at times gives me headaches.

A number of people have been continuously supportive to me, helping me update my restaurants to match today's lifestyle: Walter Wallgram, who manages Trattoria di Umberto in Whistler; Jay Paré, manager of Il Caminetto; Cosmo Piccirilli, my general manager, who has the ability to keep up with constant changes without sacrificing quality and who keeps the restaurants at the head of the line.

Special acknowledgement must be made of Bobby Copiak, Jahan Khazali, Pam Reid, Patrizio Sacchetto—in my opinion one of the finest culinary teachers—Mark Herand and Nicola Thom, and indeed every member of my staff.

In addition to my family and co-workers, friends outside the business have been very important in my life. My thanks to participants who have shared ideas in good times and bad: Jean-Claude Ramond, Joel Thibeault, Bud Kanke and his athletic wife, Dotty (who constantly reminds me to keep in shape); and colleague restaurateurs Mario Enero and Pascal Tiphine, who are always ready for a party at any time of day—their best medicine for a bout of depression.

It is important to me to thank my partners and associates, Peter Brown, Malcolm Burke, David McLean, John Tognetti, Bruce McDonald and the late David Graham and his family, for their financial and business support and their trust in me.

Also, thanks to my brother-in-law Ken Bogas and his wife, Cynthia, whom I welcome in a new venture—the restaurant Mangiamo. Ken's style of preparing food and his constant reminder that the freshest food is always the best have endeared him to me.

Names keep coming to mind and space is getting shorter, but I must not neglect to mention Attilio Gerardi, who has given me so much good advice that I consider him a benign godfather—probably the only godfather I will ever know.

And, of course, thanks to my doctors, Paul Wilson and Donald Ricci, and my trainer, Susan Rock, for keeping me healthy and sane. To Karyn Plavsic for enduring long hours of dictation, to Marlene Widas for her wizardry at the keyboard, and to editor Marilyn Sacks for her patience, my special thanks.

Well, my friends, I left the best for last—the constancy of my partner and wife, Marian, and my young son, Alessandro, who continue to show enormous patience at the long hours I keep, especially when I turn our home into a showplace for business events, cooking classes and the shooting of TV shows, even turning them out of their own home at times. And a pat on the head to my dog, Ciccio, who has shown remarkable restraint in not barking during filmings.

Whoops! Hi, Kim. I have not forgotten you. Thanks.

Contents

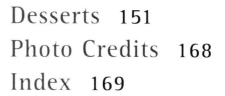

sapori

the flavour of Italy

Introduction

I was born on October 24, 1946, in Pontedera, Tuscany, between Florence and Pisa, and grew up on a typical Tuscan farm. My father, Mario, tended the vineyards, where grapes were grown for a local consortium.

My parents wanted me to become a priest; when you are young, Italians keep you pretty close to the church. They filter you to these seminaries, which are like regular high schools under the Catholic system. Then they enroll you in the priesthood.

Even as a young boy, I felt the pressure—major pressure; becoming a priest just wasn't what I wanted to do. So when I was 12, I ran away from home. It was a short run away, only a few kilometres. I remember stealing a bicycle—I just picked one up from the front of some bar. I took shelter in a small restaurant in the countryside owned by a couple who had no children. It was spring; the schools were closing; tourists were arriving. Kids at that age were all working for income, and I was looking for a job. I was lucky that they took me in. I just ran around the kitchen, washing dishes—or breaking dishes—cleaning floors, moving boxes, peeling potatoes, carrots.

After four or five days, my father came looking for me. I was sort of scared of him, so I said, "If you touch me, I'm going to run and you'll never see me again." But he just said, "Your mother wanted to know how you were doing, and you know we love you, and you can come home any time." I said, "No, I'd like to stay here and work. I want to do my own thing."

So that's how it started. Independence was my reward. I worked the whole summer and began to like the business, working around food. People were giving me a little money for tips because I was clearing the tables, setting them up, bringing bread, pouring wine. I felt needed; I felt strong. And suddenly I knew that this was what I wanted to do with my life.

Then I met a Swiss couple, who said, "You should go to hotel school, because we have a nephew who went and he's travelling the world." When I heard those words—*travelling the world*—I went in search of everything I could to find a way to get into one of these schools. Then I found out that there were government-sponsored courses, but you had to be 15 years old to get into them, and your parents had to approve.

So I had to be a good boy, go back home, finish my three years of regular school and then convince my father and mother to give their signatures so that I could enroll in the hotel course. They were still upset because I was not going to become a priest, but they saw that I wasn't going to change my mind. So my father and I took the train to Rome, he signed me into the school, gave me a little pocket money, and I was on my own.

The college for hotels teaches you everything—languages, international services, all the terminology about cooking. You are trained in a kitchen, in a dining room, for room service, how to work at a front desk, as concierge. During those three years, I was also sent to work in nice hotels in Grenoble and Geneva, returning to Rome from time to time to upgrade my courses. And I felt that I was really making progress. Everywhere I worked, people always wanted me back. The teachers from the school liked to use me for special events. When I expressed a wish to go to England, they recommended me to the Savoy in London. I was still under 20, and it was pretty exciting to be travelling on my own passport, with my own money, and having my own room.

Then, in 1967, I was working at the Hilton in London, England, and Expo '67 was opening in Montreal. The hotel sent a crew to Montreal because there was a shortage of staff there, and I came over to work at the Queen Elizabeth. There I met Alex Katz, who became the manager of the Hotel Vancouver, and after Expo he brought me to the city that was to become my adopted home.

My roommate in Montreal was also heading West, to work in a gold mine up north, and we planned to take the train together across Canada because it was cheaper than flying. Before we left, he told me, "You know, we're going to the

amichevole e divertente

friendly and fun

West, it's still dangerous, trains are still being attacked." So with my last money, I bought a cowboy hat and jeans and two guns with a leather holster—like Buffalo Bill's. After growing up watching movies about cowboys and Indians, I couldn't wait to get to the Wild West. I also bought a Yashica Super 8 camera to film the scenery, and especially the train attacks.

For days we rode through nothing but flat terrain. There were lots of telephone poles but not a single buffalo and very few cows and horses. It was depressing. So when we arrived in Winnipeg, I got out at the station for a walk wearing my cowboy hat, my holster and guns, and an RCMP officer came up to me and said, "Oh, my God, what are you doing?" When I told him my story—that I worked in the hotel business, I came from Italy, and I wanted to send a film back to my family and friends just in case the train was attacked by Indians and cowboys—he could not decide whether I was kidding or completely crazy. I can still remember the look on his face. Finally, he made me leave the guns but accepted my story and let me get back on the train. And all I had to show for the trip were sixteen rolls of flat prairie scenery, because by the time we reached the beautiful part, the Rockies, I had used up all my film.

It was in Vancouver that the world really opened up for me. By now, my constant wish was to have my own business. After working in the Hotel Vancouver for a while, I had the opportunity to buy into a delicatessen and coffee shop near the University of British Columbia. I started to do a bit of catering and began to meet people, make friends. I was doing everything—cooking, serving, making everybody laugh, kissing the ladies, acting like a nut. Someone from the University Club saw me and said, "We need somebody like you, the Club is so stiff." So they brought me in as catering manager and I met even more people, customers I still have today.

By this time, I was determined to open a restaurant in Vancouver that truly represented Italian—especially Tuscan—cuisine. At its best, Tuscany is synonymous with simplicity and freshness. There, food is thought of as "today," not "tomorrow." In Italy, the expression is: "If the garden offers us this, that's what we're going to eat today. If the market offers that, that's what we're going to have." If you start with a carrot, it still has to taste like a carrot. So simplicity and freshness in the preparation, elegance and sophistication in the presentation, and friendliness and enjoyment in the atmosphere—these were my goals.

My partner and I were now operating a place in Gastown called Casanova. It was a nice Italian restaurant, but I had a more ambitious desire. Every day on my way to work, I would pass a little yellow house on the corner of Hornby and Pacific, and in my dreams it became my restaurant.

But just then, the bottom dropped out of everything. Casanova wasn't making enough money for two partners. I was broke, and my dream seemed farther away than ever. But always, an idea comes. With my last dollars, I phoned my sister in Italy—she had a small sweater factory—and said, "Send me all the sweaters you have that are in fashion in Italy. Put them on a plane. Don't ask me why. I'll pay you when I sell them. And keep sending them until I tell you to stop." Six weeks later, ten large boxes of sweaters arrived.

I took them straight to Woodward's department store. At first, the buyer wasn't interested in taking them, but I said, "Live with them for a few days. Take them on consignment. If they sell, pay me; if they don't, I'll take them back." Two weeks later, the store phoned me. They had sold all the sweaters and wanted more. Six months later, I had made enough money to pay back my sister, put some in the bank and borrow enough to make an offer on my yellow dream house.

But by the time my first restaurant, Umberto's—the yellow house—opened, in 1973, I was broke again. Newspaper columnist Jack Wasserman had announced the opening in the *Vancouver Sun,* and by eight o'clock there was a lineup of customers. When nothing seemed to be happening, they began to get impatient, even irritated. In the kitchen, I had only one piece of veal, a box of rack of lamb, a box of tortellini and some salad makings. No wine, no liquor, no choice of dishes. My friend Francesco Alongi, who was my only helper, asked me what I was going to do. At first, I froze. Then I took a deep breath, walked into the middle of the dining room and made my confession to the crowd.

"I'm sorry, but I'm unprepared for the evening. I have enough to feed you all, but the only choice is mine. If somebody, instead of getting aggravated, could go up to the liquor store and get a bunch of wine—we'll deal with it afterwards— let's have a party. I'll cook the same for everybody. And it will be good." And everybody said, "Great idea!"

So while I was making tortellini *alla panna* and rack of lamb with a little salad, one guy goes out and comes back with five cases of Beaujolais, and the other guys serve, the ladies are all helping, everyone is getting into the act and having fun. There was an instant feeling of participation and a party mood.

At the end of the evening, they asked, "How much do we owe you? It was a great evening." I said, "Whatever you think it was worth." And everybody was writing generous cheques, not just for the value of the food but for the good time they had had.

In the following few days, the place became extremely busy and, being small, was booked solid all the time. Sometimes there were so many people I would tell them to wait in their cars and we would come and get them when a table was free, or we would bring them food. I can remember bringing a couple a piece of salami and some bread and a bottle of wine, saying, "Here's something to tide you over while you wait."

In three weeks, I went to the bank, repaid the loan and got another line of credit. Six months later, I bought myself a yellow Ferrari to match my first restaurant. From that day to this, I have opened many restaurants, and the rest is history.

In this book, I have gathered together recipes that reflect some of the memorable meals I have enjoyed with family and friends over the years. I have also tried to recapture moments involving my favourite food and memories of growing up in Tuscany. I invite you to share these memories with me.

Introduction

Wines

For this book, I wanted to present the reader with several choices of wine to accompany many of the recipes. When you select a wine to accompany your meal, I suggest that you begin by considering what characteristic of the wine will best create a harmonious balance when married with the combined ingredients of the food.

My formula is based on discovering the compatible components of both the food and the wine. An aromatic dish should be matched with an aromatic wine; a lighter meal with a less assertive wine. A dessert obviously calls for a sweeter wine, and a dish with a sweet-sour flavour weds well with a light, dry wine. With experimentation, it is possible to find that harmony that allows the bouquet of the wine to enhance the flavour and aroma of the food, and the food to complement the taste of the wine.

I have asked my friend Peter Burrow to recommend these wines not only according to their appropriateness but also according to availability. Peter has worked in the wine business for the past ten years. Previous to that, he spent twelve years working in restaurants, hotels and wine bars in Vancouver and on Vancouver Island. He is now a senior wine consultant in Canada for the wine importers Featherstone and Company and as part of his duties acts as a wine buyer for the company. In this capacity, he has travelled to the significant wine districts of France, Italy, Austria, Germany and Switzerland, as well as those in Australia, the United States and eastern Canada. (He is a graduate of the German Wine Academy in Reingau.) In addition to his oenological expertise, Peter is an avid cook. As he aptly puts it, "I clear my head in the kitchen." So who better than a fine cook and a wine expert to compile a list of suggested wines to accompany many of the recipes in this book.

Peter says that in recent years the increased interest in table wines has been the most exciting aspect of the local dining scene. No longer does such an interest have snobbish connotations. Articles about wines and vintages appear regularly in newspapers and magazines. Night school classes educate adults in the history of wines and the background of vintners. Books about wines and wine regions swell the bookstore shelves. Wine lists regularly accompany menus in even the most modest of restaurants.

I'm sure that by exploring the wines locally available to you with the help of Peter's suggestions, your meals will turn into occasions, and your cooking and dining pleasure will be enhanced. No doubt you will experience the sense of fun that Peter has discovered goes with matching a wine to a recipe and sharing that discovery with friends.

Please note that the suggested wines accompanying the recipes in this book are not to be construed as the only choices. If you can't find a suggested wine, try another. You may find an even better match.

Salute!

Appetizers

I have often wondered why Italian cuisine is so popular. Perhaps because it is accompanied by lots of hospitality, fun, wine and people. When you think of an Italian meal, you think of platters of hot steaming pastas, mounds of bread and brightly painted plates heaped with colourful vegetables, with everyone eating, drinking and (most importantly) talking all at the same time. For Italians, this scene requires a talent for ambidexterity, since as most people know, Italians need their hands in order to talk!

Amichevole e divertente—"friendly and fun"—is an Italian phrase used to describe the feelings that abound around the typical Italian table. The experience of sharing food during a meal includes warmth, simplicity, easiness; food with a high comfort level that does not intimidate anyone, either the youngest member of the family or the invited guest. You could say that Italian cuisine is unpretentious (in contrast to the image that Italians' fast red cars project).

The term *sapori*—"the flavour of Italy," or the flavour of the culture—refers to the individuality that Italian cuisine brings out. The word reflects the unique approach that each individual brings to his or her choice of the freshest ingredients in the marketplace.

With this philosophy of Italian cuisine in mind, we arrive at one of the most important parts of the meal—the antipasto, or the "dish before the meal." Antipasto dishes pay tribute to the variety of local produce and to the people who work so hard to make it available to us. These dishes consistently use the freshest ingredients of the season to visually stimulate us and sharpen our taste buds. As the seasons change, so do the herbs—and the aromas of our kitchens. Antipasto is meant to prepare us for what is to come; it acts as the precursor to the evening meal. Since antipasto is my favourite way of starting a meal, it is an appropriate beginning to this book.

A war could easily be started in Italy over antipasti. Every region claims to offer the best starting dishes. But Italians are not fighters (especially when it comes to food), so instead of taking the time to argue about whose antipasto is better, we simply sit down to eat and enjoy it. The various regions have mutual respect for their different tastes. Of course, as a Tuscan, I think we have the best—and I can unequivocally tell you that this is the truth. (Are there any other regions listening?)

Tuscan antipasto consists of the freshest of vegetables, usually grilled over a hot fire and drizzled or marinated with spicy extra virgin olive oil. Sometimes the oil is blended with aromatic vinegars and fresh herbs that are local and seasonal. Consequently, the antipasto varies with the season and the produce available at that time of the year.

One typical Tuscan antipasto dish is *Insaccati,* which consists of a variety of salami and sausage, often flavoured with *peperoncino.* This spicy red pepper, along with fennel seed, is a traditional seasoning used for flavouring the sausage and salami of the region

Another basic antipasto dish of

Tuscany is *Bruschetta,* a grilled or toasted slice of bread rubbed with fresh cloves of garlic and drizzled with extra virgin olive oil and sprinkled with salt and pepper. A sister variation of this dish is a slice of Tuscan bread spread with chopped fresh tomato and basil.

Tuscans are large consumers of *fagioli* (beans). Quite often *fagioli* are served with tuna and onions marinated in olive oil, lemon juice, and, of course, salt and pepper. You will find this dish a lot in Tuscany, where it is very much married with the "antipasto family." A dish of this kind is quite common in the countryside and in interior towns or cities.

As soon as you travel to the coast, you will find that antipasti change, with the major ingredients consisting of creatures from the sea. The most popular dish is calamari (squid) marinated in olive oil, onions, garlic, lemon juice and capers. The antipasto dishes here can include clams, mussels or any small white fish served either cold or warm but almost always with a *piccante* (savory) dressing. A seasonal herb dressing may also be used with seafood antipasto. The intention is always to stimulate the appetite.

I could go on forever about the variations in dishes to be served before the meal, but the most important thing is the sharing and the presentation—the quality of the food, not the quantity. Every region offers a tremendous choice of ingredients for both colour and texture. Use your creativity and imagination to excite your guests' taste buds.

Peperonata Braised Sweet Peppers

1   *Tbsp./15 mL olive oil*
1   *medium red pepper, quartered*
1   *medium green pepper, quartered*
1   *small onion, diced large*
    salt
    freshly ground black pepper
1   *clove garlic, finely chopped*
1/3   *cup/75 mL tomato sauce*
    (see recipe, p. 149)
1/4   *cup/50 mL coarsely grated Parmesan cheese*

Preheat the oven to 400°F/200°C.

In a medium-sized skillet, sauté the peppers and onion in the oil over medium heat for 4–5 minutes. Season with salt and pepper to taste. Transfer the peppers and onion to an oven-proof casserole dish and sprinkle with the garlic. Pour the tomato sauce over and sprinkle with the Parmesan cheese.

Place the casserole dish, uncovered, in the preheated oven and bake for 15 minutes.

Serves 2.

Note: Peperonata can be served as a vegetable side dish.

Mozzarella al forno con olive
Baked Mozzarella with Olive Toast

1	lb./500 g fresh mozzarella cheese	4	pieces of French bread sliced about ⅓ inch/9 mm thick
2	Tbsp./30 mL chopped fresh basil approximately 5 Tbsp./75 mL extra virgin olive oil salt freshly ground black pepper	4	Tbsp./60 mL black olive paste
		¼	cup/50 mL tomato concassé (see recipe, p. 145)
		4	fresh basil leaves

Preheat the oven to 400°F/200°C.

Cut the mozzarella into ⅓ inch/9 mm slices and arrange on a plate in a single layer. Sprinkle the basil over the cheese slices and drizzle with 2–3 Tbsp./30–45 mL of the olive oil. Season with salt and pepper to taste and set aside.

Brush the bread slices with the remaining 2–3 Tbsp./30–45 mL of olive oil, arrange on a baking sheet and bake in the preheated oven for 6–8 minutes, until lightly browned. Remove the toasted bread from the oven and allow to cool. Spread each slice of toast with 1 Tbsp./15 mL of olive paste and place a slice of mozzarella on each. Return the toast to the oven and bake for 6–8 minutes, or until the cheese starts to melt.

Serve on hot plates, garnished with tomato concassé and basil leaves.

Serves 4.

∧ Suggested Wine

Medium-bodied white or light-bodied red or dry rosé

Italy
Terra di Nicchie Rosato "Tenuta Tresanti" (rosé)

France
L'Estable Coteaux Languedoc Cabrières (rosé)

> Suggested Wine

Light- to medium-bodied red

Italy
La Stoppa Alfeo (Pinot Nero)

France
Chanson Givry

Canada (Ontario)
Inniskillin Pinot Noir

Crostini di tonno con formaggio
Tuna and Cheese Canapés

½–¾	lb./250–350 g fillet of fresh tuna, thinly sliced (16 slices)
6	Tbsp./90 mL butter
2	Tbsp./30 mL horseradish, drained
1	baguette of French bread, cut into 16 slices
2	Tbsp./30 mL dry red wine
3–4	balls fresh mozzarella cheese, cut into 16 thin slices (in the shape of a baguette) freshly ground black pepper

Preheat the oven to broil.

Cut the slices of tuna into the shape of a baguette slice and set aside.

Melt the butter in a saucepan. Do not let burn. Blend the horseradish with the butter, then remove the pan from the heat and keep warm.

Put the slices of bread on a baking sheet and toast slightly in the preheated oven. Remove the baking sheet from the oven and brush the bread with the horseradish butter. Drizzle the bread with the red wine. Put the tuna slices on the pieces of bread and top with the cheese slices. Return the baking sheet to the oven and broil or grill until the cheese melts.

Remove the baking sheet from the oven and put the canapés on a platter. Grind fresh pepper to taste over the top and serve immediately.

Makes 16 canapés.

Budino di pesce
Fish Pâté with Coulis of Tomatoes

1	lb./500 g fillet of any fresh white fish (cod, halibut, red snapper or sole), skin and bones removed
2	egg whites
2	cups/500 mL whipping cream
	juice of 1 lemon
	dash Worcestershire sauce
	pinch mace
	salt
	white pepper
2	bunches fresh spinach, washed and stems removed
¼	cup/50 mL dry white wine
	juice of ½ lemon
2	cups/500 mL coulis of tomatoes

Coulis of Tomatoes

8	firm, ripe tomatoes, eyes removed and with an x cut on the top
3	Tbsp./45 mL extra virgin olive oil
1	Tbsp./15 mL white wine vinegar
1	Tbsp./15 mL finely chopped fresh parsley
	salt
	freshly ground black pepper

Suggested Wine

Sparkling or light- to medium-bodied white

Italy
Zonin Prosecco (sparkling)

Spain
Castellblanch Brut Zero (sparkling)

France
Rémy Pannier Chardonnay Brut (sparkling)

Preheat the oven to 350°F/180°C.

Rinse the fillet under cold running water and pat dry with paper towels. Put the fish in a food processor or blender and process until a fine paste is formed. Add the egg whites to the processor and blend in, then transfer the contents to a bowl.

Blend the cream in the processor, then add to the first mixture. Add the lemon juice and Worcestershire sauce to the bowl and blend in by hand. Season the mixture with mace and salt and pepper to taste. Set the bowl aside.

Cook the spinach in a pot containing the wine and lemon juice for approximately 1 minute, until the spinach has just wilted. Then drain the pot and put the spinach in the processor. Add one-half of the fish mixture to the spinach and process until smooth.

Put the spinach/fish mixture in the bottom of a rectangular buttered pâté mould. Spread the remaining fish mixture on top. Put the mould in a pan of hot water that comes halfway up the sides of the mould and cover with a sheet of buttered wax paper.

Put the pan in the oven and bake for approximately 25 minutes, until the pâté is firm. Remove the pan from the oven and the mould from the water. Allow the pâté to cool, then turn out on a cutting board.

To make the coulis, blanch the tomatoes in a pot of rapidly boiling water for 20 seconds, then plunge them into a pot of cold water to stop the cooking. Peel and seed the tomatoes, then purée in a blender or food processor. Add the oil and vinegar and blend. Add the parsley and blend. Season with salt and pepper to taste.

Put ¼ cup/50 mL coulis of tomatoes on 8 individual plates. Cut the pâté into 1 inch/2.5 cm thick slices and put on top of the coulis. Serve immediately.

Makes 8 servings.

Crostini di gamberetti
Shrimp Canapés

1	lb./500 g precooked fresh shrimp, shelled (reserve 16 whole shrimp for garnish)	4	dashes Tabasco sauce salt freshly ground black pepper
2	egg yolks juice of 2 lemons	1	baguette of French bread, cut into 16 slices
¼	cup/50 mL brandy	4	black olives, sliced into 16 rings
2	Tbsp./30 mL finely chopped fresh parsley	2	lemons, cut into 8 wedges

Preheat the oven to broil.

Set 16 whole shrimp aside. Put the remaining shrimp, egg yolks, lemon juice, brandy, parsley and Tabasco sauce in a blender or food processor and process until a fine paste is formed. Season with salt and pepper to taste and set aside.

Put the slices of bread on a baking sheet and toast in the preheated oven until golden.

Remove the baking sheet from the oven and allow the bread to cool slightly, then spread the shrimp mixture on top of each slice of bread to make canapés.

Put the canapés on a platter. Garnish each canapé with 1 black olive ring and 1 whole shrimp. Garnish the platter with lemon wedges and serve immediately.

Makes 16 canapés.

Suggested Wine

Medium-bodied sparkling

Italy
Frescobaldi Extra Brut

France
Bollinger Special Cuvée

United States (California)
Schramsberg Blanc de Noirs Brut

Carpaccio
Marinated Raw Fillet of Beef

5	oz./140 g lean fillet of beef

Marinade

2	tsp./10 mL lemon juice
2	tsp./10 mL Dijon mustard salt freshly ground black pepper
2	tsp./10 mL extra virgin olive oil

freshly ground black pepper

Put the fillet of beef in the freezer until it is firm, then slice paper thin. (A slicing machine is best for this, or have your butcher slice it for you.)

To make the marinade, mix the lemon juice, mustard, and salt and pepper to taste in a bowl. Slowly add the oil, whisking constantly in the same direction, until well blended. Pour the marinade over the beef slices and refrigerate for at least 30 minutes.

Serve with freshly ground black pepper as an antipasto.

Serves 4.

Appetizers

13

Soups

I must confess that soups have never been my favourite part of a meal. I have always found them too rich and too filling to indulge in before the main course.

In Tuscany, we divide soup into three categories: *zuppa, minestra* and *consommé. Zuppa* is a thick, creamy, extremely rich soup that is served with bread for dipping. This soup originated as *cucina povera*—poor man's food. When I was young, *zuppa* was served twice a day in our home. In fact, it was forced on us. If, for one reason or another, we didn't have it for lunch, it had a habit of appearing at the dinner table.

The second category of soup, *minestra*, is best known outside Italy as minestrone. This is primarily a vegetable soup, lighter in texture than *zuppa*.

Consommé nicely rounds out the soups, usually taking the form of a light chicken broth with perhaps a bit of *contorno* (garnish). Stracciatella (literally, "little

< Artichoke Soup, *page 17*

rags") is a good example: beaten eggs, parsley and grated cheese are added to the boiling broth.

When I was growing up, it was extremely difficult for me to establish any consistent relationship with the soup of the day. I recall coming home from school on my bicycle and first circling the house to detect the odours coming from the kitchen. (Italians used to cook with the windows open, since there were no exhaust fans in those days, so you could always smell what was being prepared.) If the odour was not to my liking, I would continue on my way and hope the soup course would be over before I decided that it was safe to come home. Of course, I always had an excuse—a stomachache, a scratched knee—something to distract my parents from the leftover soup waiting for me. Invariably, my mother would say that soup was always better when warmed up, and I had to face the unwanted bowl. I will never know for sure if the family soup of the day had any connection to my leaving home at an early age.

Later, while in training at the hotel school, I was sent to Grenoble, France, to work at the restaurant La Poularde Bressanne. Here my anti-soup fetish met a formidable obstacle. Without any warning, I had joined ranks with a beautiful restaurant whose specialty was soups. I had jumped from the frying pan into the fire—or from the soup pot into the kettle.

The owner of the restaurant, Mr. Piccinini, a second-generation Italian, ate only soups—soup for lunch, soup for dinner—nothing else. Obviously, he was a connoisseur of soups. And since I had already determined that my career was going to be in the restaurant business, I had to come to terms with the soup dilemma. It was a price I was willing to pay.

As a consequence, I was presented with a great opportunity to experience the immense portfolio of soups of the world. Its vastness surprised me, especially because Tuscans had always been known throughout Italy as the soup-eaters. (*Toscana mangia zuppa* was a well-rehearsed saying.)

Well, my friends, I must tell you that my Grenoble experience did manage to convert me to the enjoyment of many—but not all—soups. And as a father of a young son, I now find myself with the shoe on the other foot. I feel an obligation not only to make soups for him but also to teach him how to appreciate their taste.

In this section, you will find some of my favourite soup recipes, the result of coming to terms with an anti-soup attitude.

Zuppa di carciofi
Artichoke Soup

¼ cup/50 mL olive oil
2 small onions, coarsely chopped
10 small fresh artichokes, stemmed,
   with the spiky tips trimmed and
   any brown outer leaves discarded
   or 14 oz./398 mL can artichoke
   hearts, drained and chopped

   sea salt
   freshly ground black pepper
12 cups/3 L vegetable broth
   (see recipe, p. 146)
¼ cup/50 mL freshly grated
   Parmesan cheese

Heat the olive oil in a large pot, add the onions and cook over medium heat until transparent. Add the chopped artichokes and salt and pepper to taste and cook over medium heat another 6–8 minutes. Add 10 cups/2.5 L of the vegetable broth, bring to a low boil, then turn down the heat and simmer for approximately 20 minutes, or until the artichokes are tender.

Transfer the soup to a blender and blend coarsely on low speed. Strain this mixture through a fine sieve. The consistency should be thick and smooth. (If the soup is too thick, add the remaining 2 cups/500 mL of broth and bring to a low boil.)

Serve in soup bowls with Parmesan cheese.

Serves 6.

Suggested Wine

Medium-bodied white

Italy
Teruzzi & Puthod Carmen

United States (California)
Robert Mondavi Fumé Blanc

South Africa
Mulderbosch Sauvignon Blanc

Zuppa d'orzo
Barley Soup

1 cup/250 mL pearl barley
2 Tbsp./30 mL olive oil
5 small onions, finely minced
2 cloves garlic, finely minced
2 Tbsp./30 mL finely chopped
   fresh parsley
¼ cup/50 mL finely chopped salt
   pork (pancetta or bacon can be
   substituted)
4 cups/1 L chicken stock
   (see recipe, p. 147)
   sea salt
   freshly ground black pepper

Soak the barley overnight in cold water. Discard any grains that have come to the surface of the water. Drain and rinse the barley under cold running water.

Heat the oil in a large pot over medium heat. Add the onions, garlic, parsley and salt pork and sauté, stirring until the mixture begins to colour, about 4–5 minutes. Add the barley and stir a few times.

Cover with the chicken stock and bring to a boil over medium heat. Cover the pot and reduce the heat to low. Simmer gently, stirring several times, until the barley is tender, about 1–1½ hours. Season with salt and pepper to taste. Add a bit more water if the soup is too thick. When done, allow the soup to sit for a few minutes before serving.

Serves 6.

Zuppa di fagioli
Bean Soup

1	cup/250 mL dried cannellini beans
1	onion, finely chopped
1	clove garlic, minced
1	stalk celery, finely chopped
1	sprig parsley, finely chopped
3–4	bay leaves
6	Tbsp./90 mL olive oil

2	dark leaves and 2 light leaves from a savoy cabbage, coarsely chopped
¼	cup/50 mL tomato paste
	sea salt
	freshly ground black pepper
8	slices coarse brown bread, toasted
¼	cup/50 mL grated Parmesan cheese (optional)

Soak the beans in water overnight. Drain and rinse under cold running water. Place the beans in a large soup pot with 12 cups/3 L lightly salted water and bring to a boil. Reduce to a simmer and cook for 2 hours, or until the beans are tender. Set aside.

In a 3 quart/3 L saucepan, sauté the onion, garlic, celery, parsley, bay leaves and olive oil until the onions become transparent. Add 2 cups/500 mL of the broth from the beans and the chopped cabbage to the saucepan. Dilute the tomato paste with 1 cup/250 mL of the bean broth and add to the vegetable mixture. Cover and cook over moderate heat for 1 hour, taking care not to let the liquid run dry.

Press half the cooked beans through a sieve and add this pulp to the vegetable mixture. Using a slotted spoon, add the remaining beans to the mixture. Add just enough of the remaining broth to make the consistency of the soup liquid but still thick. Season with salt and pepper to taste. Place the toasted bread slices in a soup terrine and pour the soup over them. Sprinkle with Parmesan cheese, if desired.

Serves 4.

> ## Suggested Wine

Medium-bodied white

Italy
Teruzzi & Puthod Terre di Tufi

France
Les Deux Rives Blanc Corbières

Greece
Boutari Santorini

Minestra di trippa e verdure
Tripe and Vegetable Soup

1½	lb./750 g tripe
1	Tbsp./15 mL olive oil
4	oz./115 g salt pork, cubed
2	small onions, chopped
2–3	cloves garlic, crushed
1	carrot, coarsely chopped
2	stalks celery, coarsely chopped
2	Tbsp./30 mL dry white wine
1	small cabbage, coarsely chopped
1	leek, white part only, chopped
3	potatoes, peeled and cubed
	sea salt
	freshly ground black pepper
¼	cup/50 mL grated Parmesan cheese

Buy the tripe already washed and boiled by the butcher. Cut into 1 inch/2.5 cm long strips. In a large pot, heat the oil and sauté the tripe, salt pork, onions, garlic, carrot and celery for 20 minutes over medium heat. Add the wine, cabbage, leek and potatoes to the soup pot. Season to taste with salt and pepper. Cover the ingredients with plenty of water, bring to a boil, then lower the heat and simmer for 20–25 minutes. Adjust the seasoning and serve hot, sprinkled with Parmesan cheese.

Serves 6.

Minestrone alla toscana
Tuscany-Style Vegetable Soup

2	Tbsp./30 mL olive oil	1	tsp./5 mL finely chopped
1	cup/250 mL diced fresh tomatoes		fresh oregano
1	cup/250 mL finely chopped onions		salt
1	cup/250 mL diced carrots		freshly ground black pepper
½	cup/125 mL diced celery	½	cup/125 mL cooked white
½	cup/125 mL diced zucchini		kidney beans
½	cup/125 mL diced unpeeled	½	cup/125 mL peeled and
	eggplant		diced potato
3	cloves garlic, finely chopped	⅓	cup/75 mL coarsely grated
½	lb./250 g ground beef or		Parmesan cheese
	ground veal	2	Tbsp./30 mL finely chopped
10	cups/2.5 L cold water		fresh parsley
1	Tbsp./15 mL tomato paste		

In a deep soup pot, heat the oil over medium heat and sauté the tomatoes, onions, carrots, celery, zucchini, eggplant and garlic for 10 minutes. Add the ground meat to the vegetables and sauté over medium heat for another 5 minutes. Add the water, tomato paste, oregano, and salt and pepper to taste and slowly bring to a boil, stirring constantly, then lower the heat and simmer for 30 minutes. Add the kidney beans and potato to the pot and simmer for another 10 minutes, until the potato is soft but not mushy. Ladle the soup into a warm soup tureen or into warm soup bowls. Sprinkle with Parmesan cheese and parsley and serve.

Serves 6.

Note: Once cooked, *Minestrone alla toscana* can be refrigerated for one week and warmed up as necessary. If the consistency is too thick, just add water. Adjust the seasoning before serving.

Soups

Scampi in brodetto
Herb and Vegetable Soup with Scampi

8   *fresh or frozen scampi*
    (about ½ lb./250 g), peeled and
    deveined (thaw, if frozen)
½   *medium onion, diced*
2   *cloves garlic, crushed*
2   *leeks, washed and chopped*
    (white parts only)
2   *Tbsp./30 mL olive oil*
4   *fillets of anchovy, rinsed and*
    mashed
1   *cup/250 mL dry white wine*
2   *cups/500 mL cold water*

2   *sprigs fresh parsley*
2   *sprigs fresh thyme*
1   *bay leaf, crushed*
1   *cup/250 mL fish stock*
    (see recipe, p. 146)
2   *hearts of butter or Boston lettuce,*
    washed and julienned
    salt
    freshly ground black pepper
2   *Tbsp./30 mL finely chopped*
    fresh parsley

Rinse the scampi under cold running water and set aside to drain.

In a medium-sized pot over medium heat, sauté the onion, garlic and leeks in the oil for 2–3 minutes, until soft and transparent. Stir in the anchovies. Stir in the wine and simmer the mixture for approximately 2 minutes.

Add the water and blend in. Season with the parsley, thyme and bay leaf. Stir in the fish stock and bring the contents of the pot to a boil.

Add the scampi and the hearts of lettuce. Reduce the heat and simmer for approximately 3 minutes. Season with salt and pepper to taste.

Ladle the soup into individual soup bowls, 2 scampi per bowl. Sprinkle with parsley and serve immediately.

Serves 4.

Suggested Wine

Light- to medium-bodied white

Italy
Ruffino "Libaio" Chardonnay

France
Michel Redde Pouilly-Fumé

Salads

When entertaining, I always include a salad with dinner, and I recommend that you do too. I find that salad is a "peacemaker" between courses. Salad clears your palate, leaving it clean and fresh, and setting it up for what is to come. Because a dinner salad is a liaison between one course or dish and another, it should always be served in small amounts and with a very light dressing. And a pleasing combination of colours among the lettuces and greens should not be neglected. Salad served at the end of a meal, before dessert, is particularly appreciated as a contrast to the spicy or heavy taste of meat. The zestiness of a light vinaigrette dressing will revive your taste buds.

As a host, I find that the salad course serves another function. It gives me an opportunity to excuse myself from the table and disappear into the kitchen. My guests will carry on their conversation, much as they do between acts of an opera or play, allowing me time to give my attention to the next course.

Some salads in this section can be served as main courses. I still advocate using a light dressing for these, since you will be consuming greater amounts. In Tuscany, salads often show up as part of the antipasto and are more popular in warm weather.

Insalata di melanzane e pomodori alla griglia
Grilled Eggplant and Tomato Salad

2	small firm eggplants (about 1½ lb./750 g), cut into ¼ inch/ 5 mm thick slices
	salt
	extra virgin olive oil
3	medium-sized ripe but firm tomatoes, halved, seeds and juice removed

	salt
⅓	cup/75 mL extra virgin olive oil
2	Tbsp./30 mL balsamic vinegar
3	Tbsp./45 mL dry red wine
1	clove garlic, minced
10–12	fresh basil leaves

Preheat a grill, barbecue or broiler.

Place the eggplant slices in a large dish and sprinkle generously with salt. Let stand for 30 minutes to allow the salt to draw out the eggplants' bitter juices, then pat the slices dry with a paper towel.

Brush the eggplant slices with olive oil on both sides and place them on a hot grill or in a baking dish under a broiler. Cook until golden and a bit charred, about 1–2 minutes, then turn over to cook on the other side.

Grill the tomatoes the same way and remove from the heat when they are coloured on both sides and a bit wilted, about 1–2 minutes.

Cut the eggplant and tomatoes into medium-sized strips and place in a salad bowl.

Season with salt to taste and dress with the oil, vinegar, wine, garlic and basil. Toss well, then let stand at room temperature for a few hours before serving.

Serves 4–6.

Lattuga mandorla e gorgonzola
Butter Lettuce with Almonds and Gorgonzola

3½ oz./100 g blanched almonds
4   heads butter lettuce
2   Tbsp./30 mL lemon juice
¼ cup/50 mL extra virgin olive oil
1   tsp./5 mL finely diced shallot
    salt
    freshly ground black pepper
7   oz./200 g Gorgonzola cheese,
    at room temperature

Preheat the oven to 300°F/150°C.

Place the almonds on a baking sheet and toast in the oven for 5–6 minutes, until they are evenly browned. Set aside.

Carefully wash the lettuce, drain and set aside.

In a small bowl, whisk the lemon juice, olive oil and diced shallot. Season with salt and pepper to taste.

Arrange the lettuce on a large plate. Spoon the sauce over, sprinkle with the almonds and garnish with thin slices of the Gorgonzola cheese.

Serves 4.

Cicorietta croccante
Chicory Salad

Dressing
¼ tsp./1 mL dry mustard
1   tsp./5 mL minced garlic
1   tsp./5 mL freshly ground black
    pepper
1   tsp./5 mL salt
1   Tbsp./15 mL lemon juice
4   Tbsp./60 mL extra virgin olive oil
2   Tbsp./30 mL balsamic vinegar
1½ tsp./7 mL thinly sliced shallots

1   chicken breast, boned and cubed
    (skin on)
1   large bunch unblemished chicory,
    washed, dried and broken into
    3 inch/7.5 cm pieces
1   bunch arugula, washed and dried

Preheat the oven to 400°F/200°C.

To make the dressing, combine the mustard, garlic, pepper and salt, lemon juice, olive oil and vinegar in a blender. Blend on medium speed until mixed. Add the shallots to the mixture and blend in.

Place the chicken on a baking sheet and bake in the preheated oven until the skin is crispy and golden brown, about 20 minutes. Pour off the fat and let cool.

Arrange the chicory and arugula in a medium-sized bowl. Pour just enough dressing over to lightly coat the leaves. Toss gently. Place the chicken cubes on top and serve on chilled plates.

Serves 4.

Suggested Wine

Crisp, light-bodied white

Italy
Friulvini Grave del Friuli Pinot Grigio

Germany
G. A. Schmitt Niersteiner "Fisherman" Dry

Insalata di arugula e pomodori essicati
Sundried Tomato and Arugula Salad

Vinaigrette

3   Tbsp./45 mL shallots, sliced paper thin
1   tsp./5 mL minced garlic
1   tsp./5 mL freshly ground black pepper
2   Tbsp./30 mL finely chopped parsley
1   tsp./5 mL salt
2   Tbsp./30 mL balsamic vinegar
⅓   cup/75 mL extra virgin olive oil

2   bunches arugula
¼   cup/50 mL oil-packed sundried tomatoes, julienned

In a small bowl, whisk together the shallots, garlic, pepper, parsley, salt, vinegar and oil. Let the vinaigrette sit for 30 minutes to allow the flavours to blend.

Wash and dry the arugula. When ready to serve, mix the arugula and sundried tomatoes in a large bowl. Add the vinaigrette and toss to coat evenly.

Serves 4.

Insalata di pomodori e cipolle dolci
Tomato Salad with Arugula and Roasted Sweet Onions

Vinaigrette

1   shallot, minced
1   clove garlic, finely minced
2   Tbsp./30 mL balsamic vinegar
5   Tbsp./75 mL extra virgin olive oil
½   tsp./2 mL salt
¼   tsp./1 mL freshly ground black pepper

4   large ripe tomatoes
2   medium onions, Spanish or red, skin on
1   clove garlic, thinly sliced
2   bay leaves
1   tsp./5 mL chopped fresh parsley
1   tsp./5 mL chopped fresh oregano
    salt
    freshly ground black pepper
1   Tbsp./15 mL balsamic vinegar
2   heads arugula

Preheat the oven to 400°F/200°C.

To make the vinaigrette, in a small bowl, whisk together the shallot, garlic, vinegar, oil and salt and pepper to taste.

Core the tomatoes and slice ¼ inch/5 mm thick. Arrange in a bowl and drizzle with half of the vinaigrette. Refrigerate for 1 hour.

Cut each onion into 8 wedges. Sprinkle with the garlic, herbs, and salt and pepper to taste and drizzle evenly with balsamic vinegar. Place in the preheated oven and roast for 8–10 minutes, until lightly caramelized and barely tender. Remove from the oven and let cool.

Wash the arugula thoroughly. Just before serving, toss with half the remaining vinaigrette. Arrange the arugula, roasted onions and tomatoes on a platter and spoon over a bit of the remaining vinaigrette.

Serves 4.

Salads

> Seafood Salad, *page 29*

Porri con sugo di pompelmo
Leeks with Grapefruit Dressing

4   *medium-sized leeks*

Dressing
juice of 1 grapefruit
1   *Tbsp./15 mL chopped chives*
2   *Tbsp./30 mL red wine vinegar*
4   *Tbsp./60 mL extra virgin olive oil*
    salt
    freshly ground black pepper

1   *pink grapefruit, peeled and seeded*

Wash and trim the leeks, keeping only the white and light green parts and discarding the rest, including the outer two layers. In a medium-sized pot of boiling, salted water, blanch the leeks for 5–8 minutes, then refresh them in an ice-water bath. Cut the leeks into quarters lengthwise and set aside.

To make the dressing, mix the grapefruit juice, chives, vinegar, oil, and salt and pepper to taste in a small mixing bowl.

Place four pieces of leek on each plate and cover with dressing. Garnish each plate with grapefruit segments.

Serves 4.

Insalata di patate e pancetta
Potato Salad with Bacon and Mustard

2   *lb./1 kg potatoes, unpeeled*

Dressing
2   *egg yolks*
2   *Tbsp./30 mL lemon juice*
2   *Tbsp./30 mL white vinegar*
1   *clove garlic, peeled and mashed*
1½ *tsp./7 mL coarse-grain prepared mustard*
    salt
    freshly ground black pepper
1   *cup/250 mL extra virgin olive oil*

4   *oz./115 g bacon, cooked and drained*
1   *Tbsp./15 mL chopped shallot*
1   *Tbsp./15 mL finely chopped fresh parsley*
1   *Tbsp./15 mL chopped fresh chives*

Place the potatoes in a pot of cold salted water, cover and bring to a boil. Reduce the heat and simmer for 20–25 minutes, or until just tender. When done, drain and cool. Do not refrigerate.

To make the dressing, place the egg yolks, lemon juice, vinegar, garlic, mustard, salt and pepper to taste and olive oil in a blender and blend at medium speed until the dressing thickens. Set aside.

Peel the potatoes and cut into 1 inch/2.5 cm cubes. In a large bowl, gently toss the potatoes and dressing together until the potatoes are evenly coated. Coarsely chop the bacon and add to the potatoes. Add the shallots, parsley and chives and stir carefully. Place on individual plates and refrigerate for approximately 30 minutes before serving.

Serves 6.

Insalata riviera
Seafood Salad

6   medium squid
12   mussels
¼   cup/50 mL water
¼   cup/50 mL dry white wine
4   Tbsp./60 mL extra virgin olive oil
8   medium prawns, peeled and
     deveined
8   medium sea scallops

4   heads arugula
1   Tbsp./15 mL finely chopped
     fresh parsley

Dressing
     juice of 1 lemon
¼   cup/50 mL extra virgin olive oil
1   tsp./5 mL capers
1   tsp./5 mL anchovy paste
¼   cup/50 mL water
     salt
     freshly ground black pepper

Clean the squid by pulling off the heads and removing the entrails. Rinse carefully under cold running water. Cut off the tentacles in front of the eyes and reserve. Make sure the mouth is discarded. Set aside.

Carefully wash the mussels under cold running water, using a brush if necessary. Put them in a pot with the water and wine, cover and steam for 3–4 minutes, until the shells open. Drain and set aside.

Heat 2 Tbsp./30 mL of the olive oil in a small skillet over medium-high heat, and sauté the prawns for approximately 1 minute on each side. Remove the prawns and set aside to cool.

Heat the remaining 2 Tbsp./30 mL of oil and sauté the scallops for approximately 1 minute on each side. Set aside to cool.

To make the dressing, combine the lemon juice, olive oil, capers, anchovy paste and water in a blender. Blend at medium speed until the mixture becomes smooth. Add salt and pepper to taste.

Rinse the arugula in cold water; dry, julienne and place on a platter or in a bowl. Add the squid, mussels, prawns and scallops and toss with the dressing. Sprinkle with parsley and serve at room temperature.

Serves 4.

Suggested Wine

Light-bodied white

France
Moreau Chablis "Domaine de Biéville"

Israel
Golan Heights Sauvignon Blanc (Kosher)

Insalata di quaglie all'indivia e funghi
Quail Salad with Endives and Mushrooms

4–6	boneless quail, 2 oz./60 g each
	salt
	freshly ground black pepper
2	Belgian endives, trimmed, washed and dried well
3½	oz./100 g champignon mushrooms, trimmed and washed
3	Tbsp./45 mL extra virgin olive oil
¾	cup/175 mL dry white wine
2	Tbsp./30 mL butter
1	tsp./5 mL balsamic vinegar
	salt
	freshly ground black pepper

Preheat the oven to 400°F/200°C.

Season the quail with salt and pepper and set aside.

Cut the endives lengthwise, julienne style, and set aside. Cut the mushrooms into thin slices and set aside.

Heat 2 Tbsp./30 mL of the oil in a medium-sized skillet and brown the quail on both sides over medium heat until golden brown, about 3–5 minutes. Place in the preheated oven for 10 minutes. Remove the skillet from the oven and skim off the grease. Add the wine, heat on top of the stove for 3 minutes and set aside.

In a medium-sized skillet, combine the remaining 1 Tbsp./15 mL of oil and the mushrooms. Cook the mushrooms over medium heat until they are golden. Add the butter and stir for a few seconds. Remove from the heat and add the vinegar. Season with salt and pepper to taste.

Arrange the endive slices on warm plates, set the quail on top and garnish with the mushrooms.

Serves 2.

⌃ Suggested Wine

Full-bodied white to light-bodied red

Italy
Rocca delle Macìe Chianti "Vernaiolo" (red)

Chile
Errázuriz Sauvignon Blanc Reserva (white)

Canada (Ontario)
Chateau des Charmes Chardonnay (white)

⟩ Suggested Wine

Full-bodied white

Italy
Sella & Mosca Vermentino di Sardegna

United States (California)
Robert Mondavi Chardonnay Reserve

Australia
Wynn's Coonawarra Estate Chardonnay

Insalata d'anatra
Duck Salad

7	oz./200 g duck breast, cleaned and with skin removed, at room temperature
	salt
	freshly ground black pepper
2	Tbsp./30 mL olive oil
1	Granny Smith apple, peeled, cored and sliced about ¼ inch/5 mm thick
½	head lettuce, washed and drained
½	cup/125 mL vinaigrette

Vinaigrette

1½	tsp./7 mL lemon juice
¼	cup/50 mL red wine vinegar
¼	cup/50 mL olive oil
	salt and freshly ground black pepper to taste

Season the duck breasts with salt and pepper. Place skin side down in a medium-sized skillet with the olive oil. Cook for 5 minutes over medium heat, turn the breasts over and cook for another 3 minutes. Remove from the skillet and place on a cutting board. Slice the meat on an angle about ¼ inch/5 mm thick. Set aside.

In the same skillet, brown the apple slices for 3 minutes on each side.

Place the lettuce in a large bowl. In a smaller bowl, whisk the vinaigrette ingredients together and pour over the lettuce. Arrange the greens on a plate, top with the duck breast and garnish with the apple slices.

Serves 2.

Tonno sott olio con cipolla e fagioli verdi
Tuna Salad with Onion and Green Beans

2   6½ oz./184 g cans of chunk light
    tuna, drained and broken into
    pieces (do not crumble)
3   Tbsp./45 mL peeled and chopped
    red onion
3   Tbsp./45 mL peeled and chopped
    sweet white onion
⅓   lb./175 g fresh green beans,
    stemmed
2   firm, ripe tomatoes, eyes removed
    and with an x cut on the top

Vinaigrette
2   Tbsp./30 mL extra virgin olive oil
2   Tbsp./30 mL vegetable oil
    juice of 1 lemon
1   Tbsp./15 mL white wine vinegar
2   scallions, chopped
    salt
    freshly ground black pepper

In a medium-sized bowl, combine the tuna and red and white onion. Gently mix together and set aside.

Blanch the green beans in a large pot of rapidly boiling salted water for approximately 5 minutes, until tender-crisp, then plunge them into a pot of cold water to stop the cooking. Cut the beans into 1 inch/2.5 cm pieces and put in a separate bowl. Set aside.

Blanch the tomatoes in a pot of rapidly boiling water for 20 seconds, then plunge into a pot of cold water to stop the cooking. Peel, seed and chop the tomatoes into 1 inch/2.5 cm pieces. Add them to the beans and gently mix together.

To make the vinaigrette, in a small bowl, whisk together the olive oil, vegetable oil, lemon juice, vinegar, scallions and salt and pepper to taste.

Pour vinaigrette over the beans and tomatoes. Add the beans and tomatoes to the tuna and onions and gently mix.

Serves 4.

salad is a peacemaker

between courses

Vegetables

Italy is one of the few countries where vegetables are served as a main course. The Italians and other Mediterranean peoples exploit vegetables to their maximum potential. During the growing seasons you will find vegetable gardens being cultivated even in the middle of cities. On a recent trip to Florence, I noticed a man cultivating his lettuce and tomatoes in the middle of a city traffic circle. River banks, balconies and rooftops lend themselves to gardening. It seems that the urge, the necessity, the challenge to provide food for one's family is still very much alive in Italy.

I recall that when my father retired from growing grapes, he and my mother moved to an apartment two blocks from the General Hospital. While my father was recuperating from a minor operation, he noticed a courtyard outside his hospital window. He asked my mother to bring a shovel on her next visit. Before anyone knew what was going on, he had planted garlic,

< Leeks with Grapefruit Dressing, *page 28*

onions, lettuce and tomatoes in this little plot of soil. Recently when I visited my family, I ate some wonderful-tasting tomatoes and onions only to discover that they came from that hospital courtyard.

North Americans have a knack for growing grass; Italians have a knack for growing vegetables. I can't remember a meal when I was growing up where there wasn't a crunchy vegetable of the season served with extra virgin olive oil and salt and pepper *(pinzimonio)*. Just thinking about it, I can taste the juices of the sliced fresh fennel, bright juicy tomatoes, strips of cucumbers, crunchy radishes, scallions and celery, the king of the vegetables. Zucchini and eggplant are often served as a main course, usually stuffed and presented in tasty dishes such as Eggplant Parmigiana and Stuffed Zucchini with Tuna. Such vegetable courses can feed a large family or gathering inexpensively and are both nutritious and filling.

These well-known Tuscan dishes change somewhat farther south, but vegetables retain a strong presence. The most popular dish of southern Italy is *Peperonata*, a selection of seasonal vegetables with an infusion of fresh rosemary, prepared like a ratatouille. As for the northern part of Italy, vegetables diminish somewhat in proportion to rice. Rice does not grow in the south but does grow in the north and is a strong staple food there, served as a main course. In Florence, *Osso buco* will be served with vegetables; in Milan, with rice.

When you shop for vegetables in the North American market, look seriously for the freshest ones. Learn to observe the leaves and roots for brightness of colour and juiciness. Try to buy a vegetable at the peak of its taste perfection, and your recipes will give you the best results. And always wash vegetables well under cold running water. This is essential to good vegetable preparation.

I must confess that in my youth I rebelled not only against soup but also against spinach. I did not become a spinach convert until it was presented to me as a fritatta (a soft, flat omelet). For some reason, children in every age have disliked the texture and taste of spinach. Now, aware of the immense value of the vitamins and iron contained in this dark green vegetable, I can eat it every day. For my 3½-year-old, I began by disguising spinach in mashed white or sweet potato. Now he asks for green mashed potatoes, not realizing what he is eating. So if you have any spinach rejecters, you can let them think that mashed potatoes always come in green.

Every internationally known dish that has the word *Florentine* in its name will include spinach, so my area of Tuscany is well represented in this book.

Finally, what I have to say about vegetables can be summed up in one sentence: Don't take your vegetables for granted; think green and live longer. Or, in Italian: *Campa centanni—100 anni* ("Live longer—100 years").

Melanzane ripiene
Stuffed Eggplant

3   large eggplants
3   Tbsp./45 mL olive oil
    salt
⅓   cup/75 mL Calamata black olives
6   fillets of anchovy, rinsed
1½ tsp./7 mL finely chopped shallot
½   tsp./2 mL finely chopped garlic
1   tsp./5 mL chopped fresh thyme
    salt

Preheat the oven to 400°F/200°C.

Cut the eggplants into halves lengthwise. With a spoon, empty out the pulp, leaving shells about ¼ inch/5 mm thick. Be careful not to rip the eggplant skin.

Coarsely chop the eggplant pulp and place it in a baking dish coated with oil. Sprinkle with salt and drizzle with 2 Tbsp./30 mL of the olive oil.

Coat the inside of the eggplant skins with oil and sprinkle with salt. (Do not over-oil.) Put the eggplant skins in a separate baking dish.

Place both baking dishes in the oven and cook for approximately 15 minutes. Remove the eggplant pulp from the oven and let cool. Leave the shells in for another 15 minutes.

Pit the olives, finely chop and set aside.

In a medium-sized skillet, add the remaining 1 Tbsp./15 mL of the oil and the anchovies and cook over medium heat until soft, approximately 3–5 minutes. Remove the skillet from the heat and add the chopped olives to the anchovies.

Mash the eggplant pulp with a fork and add to the skillet. Add the shallot, garlic and thyme and stir carefully. Season with salt to taste.

Remove the eggplant shells from the oven and let them cool, then carefully fill with the stuffing. Return to the oven and bake for approximately 5–8 minutes to allow the flavours to blend.

Serves 6.

Suggested Wine

Light-bodied, fruity red

Italy
Bolla Bardolino Superiore

France
Mommessin Beaujolais

Hungary
Hungarovin St. Stephan's Crown Merlot

Melanzane alla capraia
Baked Eggplant and Goat Cheese Fondue

4	small or 2 medium eggplants, unpeeled sea salt	2	tsp./10 mL finely chopped fresh parsley
¼	cup/50 mL extra virgin olive oil	1	tsp./5 mL finely chopped fresh basil
½	cup/125 mL crumbled goat cheese		

Preheat the oven to 200°F/100°C.

Cut the eggplants in half and use a knife to make several deep incisions lengthwise and widthwise in the pulp. Sprinkle with the salt and let sit for 30 minutes. Dry the eggplant with a paper towel.

Set the eggplant halves on a baking dish, cut sides up, and drizzle with the olive oil. Bake in the preheated oven for 30 minutes, then put under the broiler for a few minutes until well browned.

Remove the eggplant from the broiler and spread with the goat cheese, parsley and basil. Bake again just long enough to allow the goat cheese to melt.

Serves 4.

Suggested Wine

Crisp, light- to medium-bodied white or sparkling

Italy
Valdizze Pinot Frizzante Naturale (white)

France
Pierre Sparr Crémant d'Alsace (sparkling)

Australia
Seaview Brut (sparkling)

Terrina di melanzane
Eggplant Terrine

8   medium-sized eggplants
     salt
¼   cup/50 mL flour
½   cup/125 mL olive oil
½   cup/125 mL tomato sauce
     (see recipe, p. 149)
½   cup/125 mL grated Parmesan
     cheese

¾   cup/175 mL smoked mozzarella
     cheese, sliced
6   Roma tomatoes, peeled, seeded
     and diced
1   bunch fresh basil, chiffonade
3   red bell peppers, roasted
     (see recipe, p. 51)

Slice the eggplant ¼ inch/5 mm thick. Salt, then rinse the slices. Set aside.

Preheat the oven to 350°F/180°C.

Spray a terrine mould (11½ inches/ 29 cm long, 3¼ inches/8 cm wide at the top, 2½ inches/6 cm wide at the bottom and 2½ inches/6 cm high) with pan coating. Line with foil, being careful to smooth out all the wrinkles. Overlap the sides with enough foil to cover the terrine before baking.

Lightly dust the eggplant slices with the flour. In a large skillet, heat the oil over medium-high heat, then fry the slices until they are golden brown on both sides, about 10 minutes total.

Line the bottom and sides of the terrine with slices of eggplant, overlapping them slightly and extending them over the top edge by about 2 inches/5 cm. Use enough eggplant slices to completely cover the bottom.

Layer #1

Lightly spoon a bit of the tomato sauce over the eggplant on the bottom of the terrine, spreading evenly. Top with about 1½ Tbsp./ 20 mL of Parmesan cheese, then a few slices of the mozzarella, then add a small amount of the diced tomatoes and basil chiffonade. (To make the chiffonade, wash the basil, chop fine, then dry and toss until light and fluffy.) Cover this with trimmed-to-fit eggplant slices. Press this layer down evenly, using a paper towel and a rubber spatula. Repeat this layer.

Layer #2

Pat a bit of tomato sauce and a thin layer (about 1 Tbsp./15 mL) of Parmesan cheese on top of the first layer. Top with trimmed-to-fit bell peppers. Cover with eggplant slices and press down as before.

Repeat two more layers of layer #1 and one more layer of layer #2, then finish the terrine with a final layer of layer #1. Fold the foil over the top to seal. *Note:* Always remember to press each layer down before adding an additional layer.

Cover the terrine with foil and place in a pan of hot water. Put the pan in the preheated oven and bake for 45 minutes. Remove the terrine from the water and place on a baking sheet to cool, covering with a smaller baking sheet weighted with two large, heavy cans. Chill overnight before serving.

As a starter or for a buffet, serves 10–12.

Note: This terrine will keep in the refrigerator for approximately 10 days.

Timballo di melanzane e zucchini
Charlotte of Eggplant, Zucchini and Chicken Livers

2   *medium-sized eggplants*
4   *Tbsp./60 mL butter*
2   *Tbsp./30 mL olive oil*
1½ *tsp./7 mL finely chopped onion*
½ *tsp./2 mL diced garlic*
2   *medium-sized zucchini, cut into*
     ¼ inch/5 mm cubes
     (about ½ cup/125 mL)

4   *chicken livers, washed and cleaned*
     of excess tissue and fat
     salt
     freshly ground black pepper
1   *Tbsp./15 mL finely chopped*
     fresh parsley
2–3 *Tbsp./30–45 mL tomato sauce*
     (see recipe, p. 149), warmed

Preheat the oven to 400°F/200°C.

Remove the skin from the eggplants in ½ inch/1.5 cm lengthwise strips. Blanch the skin in a saucepan of boiling water, drain and set aside.

In a medium-sized skillet, melt 1 Tbsp./15 mL of butter over high heat, then add the blanched eggplant skins and sauté for approximately 30 seconds. Remove and set aside.

Brush 4 ovenproof ramekins (about 2½ inches/6 cm in diameter and 2 inches/ 5 cm high) with 2 Tbsp./30 mL of melted butter. Line the ramekins with the eggplant skins, purple sides down, leaving ¾–1 inch/2–2.5 cm of the skins hanging over the sides of ramekins. Place a slice of eggplant in the centre of each ramekin. Set aside.

Cut the remaining eggplant into ¼ inch/5 mm cubes and set aside.

In a medium-sized skillet, combine the olive oil and 1 Tbsp./15 mL of the butter and melt over low heat. Add the onion, garlic, zucchini and eggplant to the skillet and cook for approximately 3–5 minutes. Do not brown. Season with salt and pepper to taste. Remove from the heat and set aside.

Cut the chicken livers into ¼ inch/5 mm cubes, season with salt and pepper to taste, and add to the eggplant and zucchini, stirring carefully. Add the parsley and stir for a few seconds.

Fill each ramekin with the zucchini/eggplant/liver mixture, pressing down with the back of a spoon. Fold the eggplant skins over the top of each ramekin, carefully pressing them down with your hand. Put the ramekins in a baking pan and pour enough water into the pan to reach halfway up the sides of the ramekins. Bake in the preheated oven for approximately 20 minutes. Remove from the oven and let cool for a few minutes. Remove the charlottes by carefully turning the ramekins upside down onto warm plates.

Spoon warm tomato sauce around the base of the charlottes and sprinkle with additional parsley.

Serves 4.

Suggested Wine

Full-bodied white

Italy
Antinori Borro della Sala

Australia
Penfolds "Koonunga Hill" Chardonnay

Canada (Ontario)
Cave Spring Chardonnay Reserve

Melanzane alla parmigiana
Eggplant Parmesan

1   medium eggplant, unpeeled
1   egg
1   cup/250 mL half and half cream
5   Tbsp./75 mL flour
    salt
    freshly ground black pepper
    vegetable oil for frying
1   cup/250 mL white sauce
    (see recipe, p. 145)

1   cup/250 mL tomato sauce
    (see recipe, p. 149)
¼   cup/50 mL coarsely grated
    Parmesan cheese
    pinch finely chopped fresh oregano
    salt
    freshly ground black pepper
3   dashes Tabasco sauce (optional)

Preheat the oven to 350°F/180°C.

Slice the eggplant ¼ inch/5 mm thick.

Beat the egg in a bowl, then mix in the cream, flour and salt and pepper to taste. Dip the eggplant slices into the egg mixture, letting the excess run off into the bowl.

Cover the bottom of a skillet in oil to a depth of ¼ inch/5 mm. Over high heat, fry the eggplant slices on both sides until crispy and golden, approximately 5–8 minutes in total. Drain the eggplant on a cloth or paper towel.

Butter the bottom of a casserole dish, then layer with one-third of the white sauce, one-third of the tomato sauce, half the eggplant and one-third of the Parmesan cheese. Repeat, then end with a layer of sauces and cheese.

Sprinkle with the oregano and salt and pepper to taste. If you like spicy food, add the Tabasco sauce. Put the casserole dish in the preheated oven and bake for 20 minutes, until bubbling and golden.

Serve from the casserole dish or transfer to warm plates.

Serves 2.

^ Suggested Wine

Light- to medium-bodied red

Italy
Umani Ronchi Montepulciano d'Abruzzo

France
Faiveley Bourgogne Pinot Noir

Chile
José Canepa Merlot

> Suggested Wine

Medium-bodied white

Italy
Hofstätter Pinot Bianco

New Zealand
Villa Maria Müller-Thurgau

Germany
Rudolf Müller Bernkastel
"Bishop of Riesling"

Finocchio gratinato con olive
Fennel Gratin with Olive Vinaigrette

4   fennel bulbs
    salt
    freshly ground black pepper
¼   cup/50 mL coarsely grated
    Parmesan cheese

Vinaigrette
¼   cup/50 mL mixed green and
    black olives, pitted
    juice of 1 lemon
¼   cup/50 mL extra virgin olive oil
    salt
    freshly ground black pepper

Preheat the broiler or oven to 500°F/260°C.

Cut the tops off the fennel bulbs and remove any wilted layers. Slice the fennel lengthwise into ½ inch/1.5 cm thick pieces and blanch for approximately 5 minutes in a pot of boiling water. Drain and place overlapping pieces of fennel on a lightly oiled baking dish. Season with salt and pepper to taste and grated Parmesan cheese. Set aside.

To make the vinaigrette, chop the pitted olives and put them in a small bowl. Mix the lemon juice and olive oil with the olives. Season with salt and pepper to taste.

A few minutes before serving, place the fennel in the broiler or oven and cook for approximately 3–5 minutes, until golden brown. Top with the olive vinaigrette. Serve on warm plates.

Serves 4.

Funghi al forno ripieni
Baked Champignon Mushrooms

16 large fresh champignon mushrooms, washed and trimmed
1½ oz./40 g pancetta (Italian bacon), finely chopped
⅔ cup/150 mL bread crumbs
2 Tbsp./30 mL olive oil
1 Tbsp./15 mL finely chopped onion
1 Tbsp./15 mL finely chopped fresh parsley
salt
freshly ground black pepper

Preheat the oven to 400°F/200°C.

Remove the heads from the stems of the mushrooms. Using a spoon, scoop out the pulp from the mushroom heads. Set the empty mushroom heads aside. Chop the stems and the pulp coarsely. Set aside.

In a small skillet over medium heat, cook the pancetta until lightly browned. Add the bread crumbs to the skillet, mix and set aside.

In another skillet, heat the olive oil and brown the chopped mushrooms on medium heat for approximately 5 minutes. Lower the heat, add the onion and cook for another 3–4 minutes, until the onion is transparent. Add the pancetta, bread crumbs and parsley and stir carefully. Season with salt and pepper to taste.

Season the mushroom heads with salt to taste and fill with the pancetta/chopped mushroom mixture.

Arrange the heads in a buttered baking dish and drizzle with additional olive oil. Bake in the preheated oven for approximately 15 minutes.

Serves 4.

Note: If pancetta is unavailable, bacon, ham or prosciutto may be substituted.

Suggested Wine

Medium-bodied white to medium-bodied red

Italy
Antinori Chianti Classico "Peppoli" (red)

France
Château Cazal Viel St. Chinian (red)

Porri alla fiorentina
Leeks Florentine Style

4 medium-sized leeks
2 Tbsp./30 mL butter
⅓ cup/75 mL water
⅔ cup/150 mL whipping cream
salt
freshly ground black pepper

Wash and trim the leeks, keeping only the white or light green parts and discarding the rest. Quarter the leeks lengthwise and cut into 1 inch/2.5 cm pieces.

In a medium-sized, heavy-bottomed pan, melt the butter over high heat and let it brown. Add the leeks and water, lower the heat to medium and cook for a few minutes, until the water is completely absorbed.

Add the cream to the pan and raise the heat for approximately 2 minutes. Season with salt and pepper to taste. Remove the pan from the heat and stir the leeks until they are well covered by the cream. Keep warm until ready to serve.

Serves 4.

Suggested Wine

Medium-bodied white

Italy
Batasiolo Gavi

United States (Washington)
Columbia Crest Semillon-Chardonnay
Geyser Peak Semillon-Chardonnay

Caponata
Mixed Vegetables in a Casserole (Ratatouille)

1	small onion, diced large	2	medium-sized ripe tomatoes
2	cloves garlic, finely chopped	1	Tbsp./15 mL finely chopped
¼	cup/50 mL olive oil		fresh parsley
1	medium zucchini, diced into	¼	tsp./1 mL finely chopped fresh
	1 inch/2.5 cm cubes		oregano
¼	eggplant, unpeeled, diced into		salt
	1 inch/2.5 cm cubes		freshly ground pepper
2	medium green or red peppers,		
	diced into 1 inch/2.5 cm cubes		

Preheat the oven to 350°F/180°C.

Sauté the onion and garlic in the oil in an ovenproof skillet over medium heat until the onion is transparent.

Add the zucchini, eggplant and peppers and sauté over medium heat for 10 minutes. Remove from the heat and set aside.

Blanch the tomatoes in a pot of rapidly boiling water for 20 seconds, then plunge into a pot of cold water to stop the cooking. Peel, seed and chop into 1 inch/2.5 cm pieces. Combine the tomatoes with the other vegetables. Season with the parsley, oregano, and salt and pepper to taste. Put the skillet, partly covered, in the preheated oven and bake 10 minutes, until the vegetables are tender.

Serve hot on warm plates or cold on chilled plates.

Serves 2.

Note: Caponata can be served as an appetizer.

Sformato di porcini salsa alici
Mushroom Soufflé with Anchovy Salsa

1/3 lb./175 g *porcini mushrooms
(or other available mushrooms)*
1/4 cup/50 mL *olive oil*
 salt
2 *large eggs*
1/4 cup/50 mL *whipping cream*

Anchovy Salsa
20 *fillets of anchovy*
1 tsp./5 mL *finely chopped garlic*
3 Tbsp./45 mL *olive oil*
1 Tbsp./15 mL *finely chopped
parsley*
3 Tbsp./45 mL *whipping cream*

 watercress, for garnish

Preheat the oven to 350°F/180°C.

Trim the mushrooms and wipe with a damp towel or mushroom brush to clean them. Chop coarsely. In a medium-sized skillet, heat the oil and lightly brown the mushrooms. Season with salt to taste, drain and set aside to cool.

Beat the eggs and cream together, then stir in the mushrooms. Fill four ramekins, distributing the mixture evenly. Cover each ramekin with foil, set them in a pan of water, place the pan in the preheated oven and bake for 25 minutes.

To make the salsa, in a food processor combine the anchovies, garlic, olive oil and parsley and blend until smooth. In a small saucepan, heat the cream and add the anchovy mixure. Simmer for 5 minutes, stirring frequently. Keep the salsa warm.

Remove the ramekins from the oven, scraping off the crusty edges with a knife. Turn each ramekin over onto a warm plate and spoon the salsa over the soufflé. Garnish with watercress.

Serves 4.

^ Suggested Wine

Light- to medium-bodied red

Italy
Vietti Nebbiolo delle Langhe "Perbacco"

France
Duboeuf Morgon

Bulgaria
*Suhindol Sophia Cabernet Sauvignon
Reserve*

> Suggested Wine

Medium-bodied white to medium-bodied red

Italy
*Batasiolo Nebbiolo delle Langhe (red)
Rocca delle Macìe Chianti "Vernaiolo"
(red)*

United States (California)
Robert Mondavi Fumé Blanc (white)

Composta di funghi selvatici
Wild Mushroom Compote

1/2 lb./250 g *combination of mushrooms, such as morel, button, chanterelle, oyster or porcini*
1/4 cup/50 mL *extra virgin olive oil*
1/4 cup/50 mL *balsamic vinegar*
1/2 tsp./2 mL *chopped fresh thyme*
4 *roasted bell peppers, mix of red, yellow and green, julienned
(see recipe, p. 51)*
2 Tbsp./30 mL *chopped fresh basil
salt
freshly ground black pepper*

Preheat the oven to 400°F/200°C.

Trim the mushrooms and wipe them with a damp towel. If they are large, cut them into quarters. Place in a bowl and toss with the oil and vinegar.

Put the mushrooms and thyme in a large heavy-bottomed skillet and sauté over medium heat for approximately 5 minutes, until the mushrooms are tender but still firm.

Add the roasted peppers and cook for approximately 10 minutes. Add the basil and season with salt and pepper to taste. Bake for approximately 20 minutes in the preheated oven.

Let the compote stand at room temperature for 1 hour before serving. Reheat before using.

Asparagi in padella
Asparagus with Cracklings and Black Olive-Caper Vinaigrette

1   lb./500 g medium-sized asparagus,
    cut into 5 inch/12.5 cm lengths
    and tough ends removed
    salt
    freshly ground black pepper

¼   cup/50 mL tomato concassé
    (see recipe, p. 145)

Vinaigrette
1½ tsp./7 mL chopped shallots
1   Tbsp./15 mL olive oil
1   Tbsp./15 mL chopped capers
1   Tbsp./15 mL pitted and chopped
    dry-cured black olives
¼   cup/50 mL cracklings (see below)
2   Tbsp./30 mL balsamic vinegar
¼   cup/50 mL extra virgin olive oil

Bring a large pot of salted water to a boil. Drop the asparagus in the pot and cook for approximately 2 minutes, or until barely tender. Remove the asparagus and immmediately place it in ice water. When the asparagus is cool, remove it from the water and drain. Sprinkle with salt and pepper to taste. Set aside.

To make the vinaigrette, lightly brown the shallots in the oil in a small skillet over medium heat. Reduce the heat and stir in the capers, black olives and cracklings. Remove the skillet from the heat and add the vinegar and olive oil. Set aside.

Place the asparagus in a skillet and heat, turning frequently until warmed through. Remove and place on warm dishes. Spoon the vinaigrette over the asparagus and garnish with tomato concassé.

Serves 4.

Cracklings
Fat cut from uncooked pork, goose, chicken or duck

Preheat the oven to 400°F/200°C.

Cut the fat into strips about 1 inch long by ½ inch wide/2.5 cm long by 1.5 cm wide. Place in a baking dish and cook in the preheated oven for 40 minutes, stirring often. The bits of skin will slowly turn golden brown and crisp. If the fat darkens, the oven is too hot. Drain, let cool, then chop.

Leftover cracklings can be frozen.

Asparagi con la fontina
Asparagus with Fontina and Cream Sauce

2	lb./1 kg asparagus	
1	tsp./5 mL salt	
¼	cup/50 mL grated Parmesan cheese	

Cream Sauce

¼	cup/50 mL unsalted butter
⅓	cup/75 mL whipping cream
2	oz./60 g Fontina cheese, diced
	salt

Cut off the tough asparagus ends. With a potato peeler or sharp knife, trim away the outer skin. Wash the asparagus stalks gently under cold water and tie them together into one or two bunches with string or rubber bands. (Do not tie them too firmly or they will break as they cook.)

Bring 3 inches/7.5 cm of water to boil in a tall stock pot over medium heat. Add the salt and the asparagus. Cover the pot with a lid or foil and cook until the asparagus is tender, about 6–10 minutes, depending on how thick it is.

While the asparagus cooks, prepare the sauce. In a medium-sized skillet, melt the butter over medium heat. Add the cream and Fontina cheese. Cook, stirring, until the cheese melts and the cream has thickened and reduced by half, about 1–2 minutes. Season lightly with salt.

Drain the asparagus and pat dry with paper towels. Place on individual dishes with the tips facing the centre. Spoon the sauce over the asparagus and sprinkle each serving with a bit of the Parmesan cheese.

Serves 4.

Suggested wine

Asparagus is a difficult match for wine, so consider the cheese the matching item.

Italy
Masi Valpolicella Classico (red)
Ca'Bolani Cabernet Franc (red)

Carote e cipolline al marsala
Carrots and Baby Onions with Marsala and Raisins

1   lb./500 g small white boiling onions, unpeeled

¼   cup/50 mL unsalted butter

1   lb./500 g small young carrots, peeled and cut into ¼ inch/5 mm thick slices

1½ cups/375 mL dry Marsala wine

¼   cup/50 mL golden raisins, soaked in 2 cups/500 mL water for 20 minutes, drained and dried on paper towels

2   Tbsp./30 mL finely chopped fresh parsley
    salt

Bring a medium-sized saucepan of water to a boil over medium heat. Cut a cross at the root ends of the onions and add to the boiling water. Cook 3–4 minutes, then drain and rinse under cold running water. Peel the onions and remove their dangling tails.

Melt the butter in a large skillet over medium heat. Add the onions and carrots and cook, stirring, until they begin to colour, about 4–5 minutes. Add 1 cup/250 mL of the Marsala and cover the skillet. Cook until the onions and carrots are tender but still firm to the bite, about 4–5 minutes. Stir a few more times during cooking, adding a bit more Marsala if needed.

Remove the lid (at this point there should be a few Tbsp./mL of Marsala left in the skillet). Add the remaining ½ cup/125 mL of Marsala and raise the heat to high. Add the raisins and parsley and season with salt to taste. Cook for a few minutes longer, stirring, until the liquid is almost evaporated and the vegetables are golden and glazed. Serve hot.

Serves 4–6.

Vegetables

campa centanni

live longer

Peperonata aromatica
Stewed Bell Peppers and Eggplant

1	cup/250 mL diced unpeeled eggplant	2	bay leaves
	salt	4	sprigs fresh thyme
2	Tbsp./30 mL olive oil		salt
1	cup/250 mL diced onions		freshly ground black pepper
½	cup/125 mL seeded and diced	1	Tbsp./15 mL balsamic vinegar
	green and red peppers	1	Tbsp./15 mL finely chopped
1	cup/250 mL diced zucchini		fresh parsley
1	tsp./5 mL minced garlic	1	Tbsp./15 mL finely chopped
2	cups/500 mL canned Italian plum		fresh basil
	tomatoes, crushed		

Sprinkle the diced eggplant with salt and let sit for 30 minutes, then dry with a paper towel and set aside.

Heat the oil in a large skillet over medium heat. Add the diced onions and cook until they begin to brown, approximately 5 minutes. Add the peppers and zucchini and continue cooking for 5 minutes more. Add the eggplant and garlic and keep cooking and stirring for several minutes, being careful not to burn the garlic.

Add the tomatoes, bay leaves, thyme sprigs, and salt and pepper to taste. Lower the heat, cover the skillet and cook for 5–10 minutes, until the vegetables are just tender.

Remove from the heat, discard the thyme sprigs and bay leaves, and season with the vinegar, parsley and basil. Serve hot or cold.

Makes 3 cups/750 mL.

Suggested Wine

Crisp, light-bodied white or dry rosé

Italy
Bolla Soave (white)

France
Domaine St. Hilaire Côtes de Provence (rosé)

United States (Calfornia)
DeLoach White Zinfandel (rosé)

Peperoni arrostiti
Roasted Bell Peppers

Choose peppers that are firm, heavy and unwrinkled. Using a pair of long-handled tongs, place one pepper at a time in the open flame of a gas burner. Turn the peppers occasionally while allowing them to become blistered and completely blackened. If you do not have a gas stove, arrange the peppers on a broiler pan or on a hot charcoal grill, 3 inches/7.5 cm from the heat. Broil until the entire surface of each pepper is charred.

When the peppers are done, place them in a plastic bag, closing the bag after adding each one, and allow the peppers to steam inside for 5–8 minutes. Rinse the blackened skin from the peppers under cold running water. Remove the stems and seeds. If the peppers are cooked ahead, drizzle with a little olive oil and store, tightly sealed, in the refrigerator.

Roasted peppers can be served as an antipasto, a garniture or an accompaniment to meat dishes.

Vegetables

Lattughe ripiene in brodo
Stuffed Lettuce Bundles in Broth

1   small head butter lettuce
¼   cup/50 mL unsalted butter
1   cup/250 mL chopped cabbage
1   small onion, finely minced
1   small carrot, finely minced
1   small celery stalk, finely chopped
2   Tbsp./30 mL finely chopped
    fresh parsley
½   lb./250 g veal shoulder, cut into
    ¼ inch/7 mm cubes

1   cup/250 mL dry white wine
1   Tbsp./15 mL flour
½   cup/125 mL freshly grated
    Parmesan cheese
6–8 cups/1.5–2 L veal stock
    (see recipe, p. 148)
    salt
    freshly ground black pepper

(see recipe, p. 148)

Bring a large pot of water to boil and add salt.

Cut off the root of the lettuce and remove the larger outside leaves. Choose 10 of the nicest medium-sized leaves and add them to the boiling water. Cook 15–20 seconds. Gently drain and place on a large kitchen towel to dry.

Melt the butter in a medium-sized skillet over medium heat. When the butter begins to foam, add the cabbage, onion, carrot, celery and parsley. Cook, stirring a few times, until the vegetables are lightly golden and soft, about 7–8 minutes.

Add the veal and cook, stirring, until it is lightly golden, 2–3 minutes. Add ½ cup/125 mL of the wine and the flour, then raise the heat to high. Cook, stirring, until the wine is almost entirely reduced, about 2–3 minutes. Put this mixture into a food processor with 2 of the cooked lettuce leaves.

Return the skillet to high heat. When it is very hot, add the remaining ½ cup/ 125 mL of wine. Stir quickly to pick up the bits and pieces attached to the bottom of the skillet. When there are only 1 or 2 Tbsp./15 or 30 mL of thick, juicy sauce left, add it to the food processor. Pulse the machine on and off until the mixture is finely ground but not completely puréed. Transfer mixture to a bowl and stir in the Parmesan.

In a large pot, bring the veal stock to a simmer. Taste and adjust the seasonings.

Put 1 Tbsp./15 mL of the filling in the centre of each lettuce leaf and wrap, forming a small bundle. Fold the ends of the leaf under the bundle so that the filling will not escape. When all the leaves have been stuffed, place them gently in the upper part of a steamer or colander over the simmering stock. Steam the bundles for 2–3 minutes, or until tender.

Gently transfer the bundles to individual soup bowls, ladle the hot stock over them and serve.

Makes 4 servings.

Suggested Wine

Medium-bodied white

Italy
Campobello Frascati

United States (California)
Preston Viognier

France
Château de Beaucastel Châteauneuf-du-Pape Blanc

Sformato di zucchini e noci
Zucchini and Walnut Soufflé

2	Tbsp./30 mL olive oil
½	lb./250 g fresh zucchini, finely chopped
	salt
2	eggs
3	Tbsp./45 mL whipping cream
1½	tsp./7 mL melted butter

Walnut Salsa

¼	cup/50 mL finely chopped walnuts
2	Tbsp./30 mL butter, at room temperature
1	Tbsp./15 mL finely chopped parsley
1	tsp./5 mL anchovy paste
1	tsp./5 mL lemon juice
1	tsp./5 mL finely chopped fresh chervil

Preheat the oven to 350°F/180°C.

Put the olive oil and zucchini in a skillet and cook over medium heat until the zucchini is tender and lightly browned all around. Remove from the heat, season with salt to taste and set aside.

In a bowl, beat eggs and cream together and stir in the chopped zucchini. Brush the bottoms of four individual ramekins with the melted butter. Fill the ramekins with the zucchini mixture, distributing it evenly. Cover the ramekins with foil and put in a pan of water. Place the pan in the preheated oven and bake for 25 minutes.

To make the salsa, combine the walnuts, butter, parsley, anchovy paste and lemon juice in a small saucepan and whisk over low heat for 2 minutes.

Remove the ramekins from the oven, scraping off the crusty edges with a knife. Remove the zucchini mixture by turning the ramekins over onto warm plates and spoon the walnut salsa over the soufflés. Sprinkle with chervil.

Serves 4.

Suggested Wine

Medium-bodied white

Italy
Banfi Chardonnay "Tufeto"

France
Latour Bourgogne Chardonnay

Canada (British Columbia)
Mission Hill Chardonnay Grand Reserve

Pasta

Pasta—what more can be said about this dish that hasn't already been said? So much has been written about it, and done to it—from adding a simple tomato sauce to serving it with chocolate sauce—that by now many people must be pasta'd out.

I am just one of many well-travelled Italians who deplore the abuse that pasta dishes have suffered in different parts of the world. My most shattering experience occurred in the Cape Breton area of Canada. It seemed to be impossible to find a good pasta dish in the Maritimes, until someone referred me to a restaurant in Sydney, Nova Scotia, and I mentally prepared myself for a feast. The shock came when I looked at the menu. The most exciting item on it was a spaghetti sandwich, which turned out to be toasted white bread heaped with cut spaghetti smothered in a dark red sauce and topped with four little meatballs covered in cheese. This concoction was then put under the broiler until the cheese

< Tagliatelle with Prawns, *page 57*

melted and served with a second slice of toast leaning on top, like the tower of Pisa. The freshest ingredient was a sprig of parsley, which at least gave the sandwich the colouring of the Italian flag. I had to excuse myself from the table rather than face this massacre of the noble pasta. I can laugh about it now, but at the time it seriously upset me. In a time when a lot of freedom has been given to individuals, a bit of control—in the kitchen as well as in society—is not a bad thing and is highly recommended in the preparation of pasta.

I consider myself privileged to have grown up with Mamma Delia's homemade pasta and her sauces using the freshest tomatoes, the freshest basil. Nor can I forget my grandmother's baked lasagna with lean ground meat, which my sister Marietta still makes in the same way. Another favourite was the gnocchi made every Sunday with home-grown potatoes and served with lamb ragu. These dishes speak to me of tradition, which I respect. But I also believe that change can be good. Not just change for its own sake, but change for the better.

When Marco Polo brought the concept of pasta to Venice from China, it spread to every Italian city and region but changed its shape and texture to suit local tastes. Each pasta has assumed its own individuality and acquired its own culture and education.

Of the many varieties of pasta, eight out of ten times the one showing up on a menu is spaghetti. When I was playing soccer in France and Spain, the Italians were always referred to as spaghetti eaters. (We took this as a compliment.) Spaghetti is even the most fun—just ask my son, Alessandro, who loves to play with cooked spaghetti, twirling it and swinging it around in the kitchen. My nickname for him is "little spaghetti eater."

If you are of Italian ancestry, you will always be judged on your ability to cook pasta. In fact, all of your culinary abilities will be judged on the basis of this single accomplishment. Whatever your ethnic background, I must beg of you when you are working with pasta, either homemade or commercial, remember these basic rules:

1. Cook pasta only until it is al dente—firm to the bite (Umberto's law).
2. The amount of sauce used to dress pasta should be a complement—never a soup (and you already know what I think about soup).
3. The herbs and seasonings in the sauce must be well balanced, not overpowering.

For me, pasta is Life; it is Blood; it is Energy; it is Culture. I hope these recipes will give this household food the recognition it deserves.

Tagliatelle con gamberoni
Tagliatelle with Prawns

1	lb./500 g tagliatelle or fettuccine
1	Tbsp./15 mL olive oil
1	Tbsp./15 mL butter
1	Tbsp./15 mL chopped garlic
1/4	red onion, diced
1/2	lb./250 g prawns, peeled
4	tsp./20 mL finely chopped fresh Italian parsley
2	Tbsp./30 mL dry white wine

	juice of 1/2 lemon
	salt
	white pepper
1	tsp./5 mL chopped fresh dill
1	tsp./5 mL chopped fresh fennel
1	tomato, seeded and cut into julienne slices
2	Tbsp./30 mL butter

Cook the pasta al dente in a large amount of boiling salted water: 3–5 minutes for fresh tagliatelle or fettuccine; 5–7 minutes for packaged. Drain and set aside.

In a large sauté pan or skillet, heat the oil and butter over medium heat. Add the garlic and onion and sauté until soft. Add the prawns and 2 tsp./10 mL of the parsley and cook for 2 minutes. Add the wine and lemon juice. Season with salt and pepper to taste.

Add the cooked pasta to the pan together with the dill, fennel, tomato and butter. Mix well and heat over medium heat for 2–3 minutes. Serve in a large bowl, sprinkled with the remaining chopped parsley.

Serves 4.

Suggested Wine
Medium-bodied white

Italy
Ducugnano dei Barbi Orvieto Classico

Germany
G. A. Schmitt Niersteiner Schloss Schwabsburg Riesling Kabinett

South Africa
Bouchard Finlayson Sauvignon Blanc

Pasta all'uovo
Basic Egg Pasta

1½	cups/375 mL extra fine durum semolina flour
2	eggs

Place the flour on a pastry board or in a large mixing bowl. Make a well in the centre of the flour and crack the eggs into the well. Using a fork, beat the eggs, drawing the flour into the eggs a little at a time. If other ingredients are called for in your recipe, they may be added at this time.

When the dough begins to hold together and the eggs are completely absorbed into the flour, it is ready to be kneaded. If you are using a bowl, move the dough onto a flat surface. Flour your hands lightly. Work the dough with your hands until it forms a ball. Discard any bits of flour or dough that have not been absorbed into the dough. Knead for 5 minutes, pulling the dough towards you and then pressing it away from you with the heels of your hands, rotating the dough a quarter turn between each fold. You may have to add a little bit of flour to the dough and/or your hands during this time if the dough starts to stick. After you have finished kneading, and the dough is nice and smooth, wrap it in a clean, damp kitchen towel and let it rest for 10 minutes.

Cut on a cutting board, using a sharp knife or a serrated dough cutter, according to the requirements of the recipe.

Makes approximately 1 lb./500 g.

Linguine al limone e fagiolini verdi
Linguine with Green Beans and Lemon Sauce

1   lb./500 g linguine
½   lb./250 g fresh green beans
½   cup/125 mL whipping cream
½   cup/125 mL yogurt
1   Tbsp./15 ml grated lemon rind
½   cup/125 mL coarsely grated Parmesan cheese
    salt
    freshly ground black pepper
1   Tbsp./15 mL finely chopped fresh chives

Cook the pasta al dente in a large amount of boiling salted water: 3–5 minutes for fresh linguine; 5–7 minutes for packaged or frozen.

Blanch the green beans in boiling salted water for 2 minutes. Drain and rinse under cold running water. Cut the beans into 1 inch/2.5 cm lengths and set aside.

In a large saucepan, combine the cream, yogurt and grated lemon. Add the green beans and cook over medium heat for 2 minutes. Add the linguine and toss gently while gradually adding the Parmesan cheese. Add salt and pepper to taste. Sprinkle with chives and serve on warm plates.

Serves 4–6.

^ Suggested Wine

Crisp, light white

Italy
Pasqua Soave

France
Sauvion et Fils Muscadet les Ormeaux

Canada (British Columbia)
Gehringer Bros. Johannisberg Riesling

> Suggested Wine

Light- to medium-bodied white

Italy
Campobello Frascati

United States (Washington)
Columbia Winery Semillon

United States (Oregon)
King Estate Pinot Gris

Penne al cavolfiore
Penne with Cauliflower

1   lb./500 g penne
½   lb./250 g cauliflower flowerettes
4   Tbsp./60 mL olive oil
½   cup/125 mL pitted and finely chopped Calamata black olives
7   fillets of anchovy, rinsed and chopped
    salt
    freshly ground black pepper

Cook the pasta al dente in a large amount of boiling salted water: 3–5 minutes for fresh penne; 5–7 minutes for packaged or frozen.

In boiling salted water, cook the cauliflower flowerettes for 5 minutes, then cool under cold running water. Dry with a paper towel and set aside.

In a large skillet, combine the oil, cauliflower, olives and anchovies and sauté over medium heat for 5 minutes. Add the penne and toss for a few seconds.

Add salt and pepper to taste and serve on a warm platter.

Serves 4.

Tagliolini con pollo e asparagi
Tagliolini with Chicken and Asparagus

8	oz./250 g fresh tagliolini or
	12 oz./350 g packaged tagliolini
1	chicken breast, skin removed
	salt
4	Tbsp./60 mL olive oil
2	Tbsp./30 mL butter
1	shallot, thinly chopped

12	fresh asparagus tips, blanched
¼	cup/50 mL whipping cream
¼	cup/50 mL chicken stock
	(see recipe, p. 147)
1	tsp./5 mL finely chopped
	fresh parsley
	grated Parmesan cheese (optional)

Cook the pasta al dente in a large amount of boiling water: 3–5 minutes for fresh tagliolini, 5–7 minutes for packaged. Drain and set aside.

Season the chicken breast with salt. In a small skillet, heat 3 Tbsp./45 mL of the olive oil and brown the breast on both sides for about 5 minutes. Cool and slice about ½ inch/1.5 cm thick. Set aside.

In a medium-sized skillet, combine the butter, remaining 1 Tbsp./15 mL of olive oil and shallot and cook over medium heat until the shallot is transparent. Stir in the chicken slices and the asparagus tips. Add the cream and chicken stock and cook for 1–2 minutes.

Toss the tagliolini in a bowl with the asparagus and chicken. Sprinkle with parsley and, if desired, grated Parmesan.

Serves 2.

Suggested Wine

Full-bodied white or light-bodied red

Italy
Rocca delle Macìe Chianti "Vernaiolo" (red)

Israel
Golan Heights Sauvignon Blanc (Kosher) (white)

France
Fortant de France Merlot (red)

Ravioli di melanzane al burro fuso
Eggplant Ravioli with Butter

1	lb./500 g basic egg pasta (see p. 57)

Filling

1 lb./500 g eggplant
   salt
1 tsp./5 mL butter
1 tsp./5 mL olive oil
2 cloves garlic, finely chopped

1 small onion, finely chopped
2 medium-sized ripe tomatoes
8 basil leaves
¼ cup/50 mL goat cheese

3 Tbsp./45 mL butter
4 sprigs parsley, finely chopped

Peel and slice the eggplant, sprinkle with salt and place in a colander. Leave for 1 hour to draw out the bitter juices. Rinse and dry. Finely chop and set aside.

Heat the butter and oil over medium heat in a medium-sized saucepan. Add the garlic and onion and fry for a few minutes.

Blanch the tomatoes in a pot of rapidly boiling water for 20 seconds, then plunge into a pot of cold water to stop the cooking. Peel, seed and chop the tomatoes into 1 inch/2.5 cm pieces. Add to the garlic and onion together with the basil. Cook for about 15 minutes.

Add the eggplant and cook until the mixture reaches the consistency of a thick paste. Mix in the goat cheese. Set aside.

Ravioli

Using a rolling pin, roll out the egg pasta dough on a floured surface into a sheet as thin as possible without breaking the dough. Cut the sheet into two 6 inch x 12 inch/15 cm x 30 cm pieces. Set one piece aside and cover it with a wet towel. Using a knife, mark the remaining sheet in 2 inch/5 cm squares, making 18 squares. Drop the eggplant mixture by the teaspoonful in the centre of each square. Brush the edges of the sheet with water, then place the second sheet over the filled sheet. Press down the edges to seal. Using a rolling cutter, cut the ravioli into 18 squares.

Dust a baking sheet with flour and place the individual ravioli on it. Let them dry for 1 hour before cooking. Cook the ravioli in plenty of boiling salted water for 5 minutes.

Melt 3 Tbsp./45 mL butter in a saucepan. Drain the pasta and transfer to a warm serving platter. Pour the melted butter over the ravioli and garnish with parsley.

Serves 4.

Suggested Wine

Medium-bodied red

Italy
Duca di Salaparuta Corvo Rosso

Portugal
Fonseca Periquita

South Africa
Kleindal Pinotage

Pansoti con salsa di noci alla ligure
Ravioli with Walnut Sauce

Filling

10	oz./300 g fresh spinach
1	medium clove garlic, minced
1	egg
¼	cup/50 mL ricotta cheese
2	Tbsp./30 mL grated Parmesan cheese
1	tsp./5 mL sea salt
	freshly ground black pepper

Ravioli

3	cups/750 mL extra fine durum semolina flour
½	cup/125 mL dry white wine
	pinch salt

Walnut Sauce

1	slice fresh or day-old white bread, ½ inch/1.5 cm thick, crusts removed
½	cup/125 mL milk
⅔	cup/150 mL walnut pieces
½	cup/125 mL buttermilk
2	Tbsp./30 mL olive oil
2	Tbsp./30 mL grated Parmesan cheese

Suggested Wine

Medium- to full-bodied white

Italy
Antinori Borro della Sala

France
Labouré-Roi Pouilly-Fuissé

Australia
Penfolds "Koonunga Hill" Semillon-Chardonnay

To make the filling, wash the spinach in cold water, then blanch in boiling salted water. Drain and squeeze out excess water.

In a medium–sized bowl, combine the spinach, garlic, egg, ricotta and Parmesan cheese until well blended. Season to taste with the salt and pepper. Set aside.

To prepare the ravioli, mix the semolina flour, wine and salt in a large bowl. Add enough water to make a smooth dough. On a flat surface, knead the dough well, then roll evenly with a rolling pin into a thin sheet. Cut into 2 inch/5 cm squares.

Put a small amount of spinach filling on each square, brush the edges of the pasta with water, fold to make a triangle and press the edges to seal the dough.

To make the sauce, soak the bread in the milk. Put the walnuts and soaked, squeezed bread in a food processor, add the buttermilk and oil and purée until the mixture is smooth. Put the purée in a medium-sized pot over medium heat. Warm, stirring constantly to prevent sticking, then remove from the heat and keep warm.

Cook the ravioli in a large pot of salted water until tender, approximately 10–12 minutes. Drain and transfer to a warm platter. Spoon the walnut sauce over, sprinkle with Parmesan cheese, toss and serve.

Serves 4.

Fettucine con fiori di zucca e gamberoni
Fettuccine with Zucchini Flowers and Prawns

1 lb./500 g fettuccine	freshly ground black pepper
20–25 zucchini flowers	⅓ cup/75 mL whipping cream
1 lb./500 g fresh prawns	1 Tbsp./15 mL finely chopped fresh parsley
2 Tbsp./30 mL butter	
¼ cup/50 mL olive oil	fresh chervil
1 medium shallot, finely chopped	Parmesan cheese (optional)
salt	

Cook the pasta al dente in a large amount of boiling salted water: 2–3 minutes for fresh fettuccine; 5–7 minutes for packaged. Drain and set aside.

Clean the zucchini flowers, discarding the pistils. Cut each flower into 4 pieces lengthwise. Keep some pieces aside for garnish. Peel and wash the prawns under cold running water. Dry with paper towels and set aside.

In a large pan over medium heat, melt the butter and add the olive oil. When the butter and oil start bubbling, add the shallot and zucchini flowers. Cook for 5 minutes until all are lightly browned. Add the prawns and cook for 3 minutes. Season with salt and pepper to taste. Add the cream and bring to a boil. Add the fettuccine and the parsley and toss gently until the pasta is well coated with the sauce. Serve on warm plates, garnished with the reserved zucchini flowers and the chervil.

If desired, sprinkle with Parmesan cheese.

Serves 4–6.

Suggested Wine

Medium- to full-bodied white

Italy
Teruzzi & Puthod Terre di Tufi

Germany
G. A. Schmitt Niersteiner Pinot Blanc Rheinhessen

France
Rothschild Mouton Cadet Blanc

Fettucine gorgonzola
Fettuccine with Gorgonzola

1   lb./500 g fettuccine

Sauce
1½ cups/375 mL whipping cream
6   oz./170 g Gorgonzola cheese
2   Tbsp./30 mL butter
    salt
    freshly ground black pepper

½   cup/125 mL coarsely grated
    Parmesan cheese
¼   cup/50 mL finely chopped
    fresh parsley

Cook the pasta al dente in a large amount of boiling salted water: 2–3 minutes for fresh fettuccine; 5–7 minutes for packaged.

Heat the cream in a large skillet over medium heat until it begins to bubble. Crumble the Gorgonzola cheese into the cream, add the butter and heat until the cheese has melted. Season with salt and pepper to taste. Add the fettuccine to the cheese mixture. Toss and heat.

Serve the fettuccine in a warm serving bowl or on warm plates, sprinkled with Parmesan cheese and parsley.

Serves 4–6.

Suggested Wine

Rich, full-bodied white to medium-bodied red

Italy
Renato Ratti Nebbiolo d'Alba "Ochetti" (red)

France
Bouchard Père et fils Beaune du Château Premier Cru (white)

United States (California)
Caymus Vineyards Conundrum (white)

Fettucine al funghetto
Fettuccine with Mushrooms

1   lb./500 g fettuccine

Sauce
2   cups/500 mL champignon or
    chanterelle mushrooms
3   Tbsp./45 mL olive oil
1   clove garlic, shaved
¼   cup/50 mL butter
1   Tbsp./15 mL finely chopped
    fresh parsley

    salt
    freshly ground black pepper
¼   cup/50 mL whipping cream

6   fresh basil leaves, for garnish
½   cup/125 mL finely grated
    Parmesan cheese

Cook the pasta al dente in a large amount of boiling salted water: 2–3 minutes for fresh fettuccine; 5–7 minutes for packaged.

Wash the mushrooms and dry them with a cloth or paper towel, then slice.

Put the olive oil and garlic in a large skillet and sauté over medium heat until the garlic is lightly browned, then add mushrooms and sauté for 3–5 minutes, until the mushrooms are light brown. Add butter and parsley to the skillet and season with salt and pepper to taste. Add the cream and heat for a few seconds, then add the fettuccine and toss. Serve on warm plates and garnish with basil leaves. Serve Parmesan cheese on the side.

Serves 4–6.

Suggested Wine

Full-bodied white to medium-bodied red

Italy
*Castellare di Castellina Chianti Classico
(red)*

Spain
*Torres Don Miguel Torres Reserva
Especial (red)*

New Zealand
Wairau River Sauvignon Blanc (white)

Fettucine con uovo all'olio di tartufo
Fettuccine with Egg and Truffle Oil

1   lb./500 g fresh fettuccine
    (see below)
½   cup/125 mL butter, at room
    temperature
4   egg yolks
4   tsp./20 mL white truffle oil

Cook the fettuccine in a large amount of boiling salted water for 2–3 minutes.
In the meantime, add the butter to a small skillet and cook until light brown, then
set aside. Drain the pasta when done and divide equally among 4 warm shallow
soup bowls. Pour the melted butter over the fettuccine and place an egg yolk on
top of each serving. Pour 1 tsp./5 mL of truffle oil over each bowl and serve.

Serves 4.

Fettuccine
Make the basic egg pasta recipe on p. 57, then roll out the dough about ¹⁄16 inch/
1.5 mm thick on a floured surface, being careful not to let the dough stick. (Lift
gingerly and sprinkle flour under the dough to prevent sticking.) Allow the dough
to rest 15 minutes. Roll up the dough in jelly-roll fashion and cut horizontally into
¼ inch/5 mm strips. Unroll the strips, then proceed with the recipe.

Suggested Wine
Medium-bodied white

Italy
Ceretto Arneis "Blange"

France
Antonin Rodet Rully Blanc "Château de Rully"

United States (Washington)
Paul Thomas Columbia Winery Chardonnay

Pasta

pasta is life

it is energy, culture

Lasagne Mamma Delia
Mamma Delia's Lasagna

1	Tbsp./15 mL olive oil	1¼	cups/250 mL white sauce
4	tsp./20 mL salt		(see recipe, p. 145)
4	qt./4 L cold water	4	cups/1 L meat sauce
1	lb./500 g fresh lasagna noodles		(see recipe, p. 148)
	(or 1½ lb./750 g packaged lasagna)	2	cups/500 mL coarsely grated
2	Tbsp./30 mL butter		Parmesan cheese

Preheat the oven to 300°F/150°C.

Add the oil and salt to the water in a 5 quart/5 L pot (the oil prevents the noodles from sticking). Bring the water to a boil over high heat and add the lasagna noodles. Cook al dente: 3–5 minutes for fresh pasta; 5–7 minutes for packaged lasagna. Drain and rinse with cold running water. Set aside.

Spread the butter and ¼ cup/50 mL of the white sauce in the bottom of a 16 x 12 x 3 inch/40 x 30 x 7.5 cm baking pan. Put one layer of lasagna noodles on top of the sauce. Spread 1 cup/250 mL of the meat sauce on top of the noodles. Spread ¼ cup/50 mL of the white sauce on top of the meat sauce. Sprinkle ½ cup/125 mL of the Parmesan cheese on top of the white sauce. Cover the cheese with another layer of lasagna noodles. Repeat until there are four layers, ending with Parmesan cheese on top. Put the baking dish in the preheated oven and bake for 30 minutes.

Serve on warm plates.

Serves 6–8.

^ Suggested Wine

Medium- to full-bodied red

Italy
Fattoria dei Barbi Brusco dei Barbi

United States (California)
Sebastiani Vineyards Barbera

Australia
Chateau Tahbilk Shiraz

> Suggested Wine

Medium- to full-bodied red

Italy
Rocca delle Macìe Chianti Classico Riserva

Chile
Cousiño Macul Cabernet Sauvignon "Antiguas Reservas"

Maccheroni all'anatra
Macaroni with Duck Breast

1	lb./500 g macaroni

Duck Sauce

1	lb./500 g duck breast, skin removed
1	Tbsp./15 mL butter
2	Tbsp./30 mL olive oil
1	clove garlic
1	medium shallot, finely chopped
1	sprig fresh rosemary
1	bay leaf
1	cup/250 mL chicken stock (see recipe, p. 147)
1	Tbsp./15 mL flour (for thickening)
4	sprigs fresh sage, chopped

Cook the pasta al dente in a large amount of boiling salted water: 3–5 minutes for fresh macaroni; 5–7 minutes for packaged. Drain and set aside.

Cut the duck breast into cubes. In a medium-sized skillet, melt the butter and oil over high heat. Add the diced duck and brown for 5–8 minutes. Add the garlic, shallot, rosemary and bay leaf. Cook for 10 more minutes, until the duck breast is well browned. Stir in the chicken stock. Add the flour and stir until the sauce is smooth and creamy.

Add the macaroni to the duck sauce, toss and heat. Serve on hot plates and garnish with sage.

Serves 4.

Cannelloni alla fiorentina
Cannelloni Stuffed with Meat and Spinach

30 fresh pasta squares
(see recipe for egg pasta, p. 57),
cut 4 inches/10 cm square

Filling
1 Tbsp./15 mL butter
3 lb./1.5 kg ground veal
2 bunches fresh spinach
¾ cup/175 mL cold water
1 large onion, ground in a food
grinder or food processor
1 tsp./5 mL olive oil
1 tsp./5 mL butter
1 large carrot, grated
2 stalks celery, finely chopped

3 cloves garlic, minced
4 eggs
3 cups/750 mL white sauce
(see recipe, p. 145)
1 cup/250 mL coarsely grated
Parmesan cheese
¼ cup/50 mL fine bread crumbs
salt
freshly ground black pepper
pinch nutmeg

1 cup/250 mL whipping cream
1 cup/250 mL coarsely grated
Parmesan cheese

Cook the fresh pasta al dente in a large amount of boiling salted water, 3–5 minutes. Drain and set aside.

Sauté the ground veal in butter in a large skillet on medium heat for 5 minutes, until the veal turns white, then put in a bowl and set aside.

Wash and stem the spinach, discarding any limp or discoloured leaves. Bring the water to a boil. Steam the spinach, covered, for 3–4 minutes, then drain and rinse with cold running water. Remove as much water as possible from the spinach by squeezing it by hand, then dry with a clean cloth. Finely chop the spinach, then add to the ground veal and mix thoroughly.

In another skillet, sauté the onion in the oil and butter over medium heat until the onion is transparent, about 5 minutes. Add the carrot, celery and garlic to the onion and sauté over medium heat for 5 minutes, then add this mixture to the ground veal/spinach mixture and combine. Add the eggs, 1 cup/250 mL of the white sauce, Parmesan cheese, bread crumbs, salt and pepper to taste and nutmeg and mix thoroughly.

Preheat the oven to 350°F/180°C.

Put a portion of the filling on each pasta square and roll up. Cover the bottom of a casserole with the cream and put the cannelloni side by side in the dish. Cover with the remaining 2 cups/500mL of the white sauce and Parmesan cheese and bake in the preheated oven for 30 minutes until bubbling.

Serve on warm plates.

Makes 30 rolls.

Note: Make this recipe ahead and freeze some of the cannelloni.
(Cook more pasta squares than necessary; some may tear during cooking.)

Suggested Wine

Medium-bodied red

Italy
Travignoli Chianti Rufina

Spain
Bodegas Monticello Viña Cumbrero Crianza

Lebanon
Château Musar

Pasta

72

Linguine al pesto
Linguine with Pesto Sauce

1	lb./500 g linguine

Pesto Sauce

2   cups/500 mL fresh basil
    (stems and leaves), packed
½   cup/125 mL pine nuts
2   medium cloves garlic
½   cup/125 mL freshly grated
    Parmesan cheese
¼   cup/50 mL freshly grated Romano
    cheese
½   cup/125 mL olive oil

2   Tbsp./30 mL unsalted butter
    (optional)
    pinch salt
½   cup/125 mL chicken stock
    (see recipe, p. 147)
1   Tbsp./15 mL unsalted butter

½   cup/125 mL freshly grated
    Parmesan cheese
4–6 sprigs fresh basil

Cook the pasta al dente in a large amount of boiling salted water: 3–5 minutes for fresh linguine; 5–7 minutes for packaged. Drain and set aside.

To make the sauce, put the basil, pine nuts, garlic, cheeses, olive oil, butter and salt in a blender or food processor and blend thoroughly. Put the pesto sauce in a large skillet and cook over medium-low heat. Stir in the chicken stock and butter until well blended, then simmer for approximately 5 minutes.

Add the linguine to the sauce. Toss and heat.

Serve the linguine on a warm serving platter or warm plates. Sprinkle with Parmesan cheese. Garnish with sprigs of fresh basil.

Serves 4–6.

Suggested Wine

Medium-bodied white

Italy
Friulvini Tocai Grave del Fruili

United States (California)
Mirassou Pinot Blanc

New Zealand
Nobilo White Cloud

Fish and Seafood

Seafood has always excited me. It is adaptable to almost any method of cooking—baking, pan-frying, poaching, steaming, grilling—and is even good marinated and served cold. In most places it is available year-round. And it is healthful, a food for today's lifestyle.

Before Garibaldi united Italy into one country, it was a region of many separate states, and each state was known for its own local produce or catch of the sea. When Italy became a republic, the country turned into a market basket where food was shared from south to north, from east to west, from the seacoast to the interior regions. Today you are more likely to find the freshest seafood in Milan than in such ports as Genoa or Venice because food in today's market economy moves according to supply and demand, and Milan is one of the largest financial centres of Italy.

But Italians everywhere love seafood. After all, Italy's coastline extends for 600 miles (almost 1000 km) from

< Orange Roughy with Pesto, *page 81*

the Ligurian Sea to the Mediterranean and up the Adriatic. The problem lies not with accessibility but with the condition of one's pocketbook. Since seafood is expensive to catch and to transport, it is not an everyday table food except on Friday, when it makes its appearance religiously in one form or another in every household.

In Tuscany, our Friday meal was always predictable: *Baccalà*, a salted dry cod that had been soaked in water for twenty-four hours to soften it and make it less salty. A variation of this dish was eaten throughout Europe for centuries because it did not require refrigeration. Tuscans still claim *Baccalà* as one of the most ancient and rustic of country dishes, and it is still the primary food at every important celebration or event, such as the grape harvest, where it is as traditional as turkey at an American Thanksgiving.

In 1974, I was chosen to represent Canada at an international culinary convention, Gran Collar Gastronomico Internacionale, in Madrid. The restaurateurs' achievements were celebrated with special dishes prepared by the host country, Spain. Among the presentations, the dish that stood out above others for me was *Baccalà*. Each Spanish province offered this salted codfish in one form or another, which heightened its respectability in my eyes. (Of course, it goes without saying that my mother's recipe is the best.)

I first tasted seafood, other than salt cod, when my career took me to Milan, where I found an abundance of Adriatic and Mediterranean seafood as well as freshwater fish from the many lakes in the area. Spectacular seafood restaurants flourished, and expensive dishes were always available because there was money to pay for them. No other city in Italy offers such a range of seafood.

One of the dishes I especially recall, served in the restaurant Massimo on Via Magenta, was *Zuppa da gambero rosso*, a delicious light crayfish bisque. Baby crayfish were fished from the local creeks at night. Many times, I joined the chef on these fishing expeditions, carrying a piece of prosciutto in my pocket as bait. The secret of the recipe, I learned, was to cook the crayfish while they were still alive and active.

Another seafood dish found in many places around the world is calamari, which is especially well represented in Greek communities, where it is most often served deep-fried. In Italy, calamari is recognized as a national dish and is prepared in a thousand different ways. In 1973, when I opened the original Umberto's, I decided to call calamari by its proper name—squid. The story I am about to tell you is not a fish tale but a fish-marketing tale.

After six months of operation, not one dish of squid had been ordered in my dining room. It took me that long to realize that my patrons did not connect squid with calamari. It was definitely time to change the presentation. I decided to offer what in Italy is called *Calamari ripieni*—the squid is stuffed (taking on the shape of a small bird) and baked. When I put this dish on the menu and called it Florentine Bird, it outsold every other item by 80 per cent.

Seafood can be enjoyed in many different ways and circumstances, even as a "dish of the moment." Late one afternoon, friends and I were taking a drive in

New Brunswick, just north of Moncton. We noticed that there were lobster traps everywhere, and the idea of buying our dinner fresh from the lobster man was compelling. After stopping to buy a serrated knife and paper plates, we returned to the beach, bought our lobsters, made our fire from dry driftwood and proceeded to have a two-hour feast. Every ingredient was there for a memorable dinner, even abundant water for the cleanup—no serviettes necessary. So if you happen to be in the right place at the right time, just let the fish jump from the water into the fire, whether it be lobster, salmon, trout or whatever. You can enjoy a most memorable dinner with utilitarian means and utensils, and it will be as worthy as one in the finest Milan restaurant.

The best tip I can give you for selecting seafood is that the fish should smell fresh—it should not have a strong odour. When buying a whole fish, make sure that the eyes are bright and shiny and the skin and gills vibrant, not dull. And fish should always be firm to the touch.

For best results in cooking, buy seafood that is in season, cook it the same day you buy it, and never, never overcook it. Only then will its three most important qualities—tenderness, moistness and sweetness—be retained.

Seafood is rich in essential vitamins and nutrients. All of us would benefit by eating more of this healthful food. In this book, you will find not only my favourite recipes but also those using fish available in your local markets. Don't be afraid to use your own creativity and flair in preparing seafood; you will be amply rewarded.

Triglie al cartoccio
Red Mullet in Papillote

4   large fresh red mullet (or 4 fillets
    of red snapper)
4   cloves garlic, minced
1   bay leaf
    olive oil
    salt
½   tsp./2 mL fennel seeds

Preheat the oven to 425°F/220°C.

Clean the fish carefully, rinse and pat dry with paper towels. If the mullet are fresh, gut them but leave the liver inside. It is less bitter than the liver of other fish and is considered something of a delicacy.

Place each fish on a piece of wax paper or foil and season inside and out with the garlic, bay leaf, oil and salt to taste. Sprinkle the fish with the fennel seeds. Fold over the edges of the paper or foil, place in a pan and bake in the preheated oven for about 20 minutes, or until the parcel looks inflated and the fish inside is cooked through.

Serves 4.

Suggested Wine

Crisp, medium-bodied white

Italy
Pio Cesare Cortese di Gavi

South Africa
Mulderbosch Sauvignon Blanc

Spain
Bodegas Palacio Cosme Palacio Blanco

Filetti di persico e cipolle agrodolce
Ocean Perch with Sweet and Sour Onions

½   lb./250 g onions, thinly sliced
1⅓ cups/325 mL dry red wine
¼   cup/50 mL red wine vinegar
¾   cup/175 mL water
2   Tbsp./30 mL honey
2   Tbsp./30 mL butter
     salt
     freshly ground black pepper

4   fillets of fresh perch (or sea bass),
     7 oz./200 g each, skinned
     salt
     freshly ground black pepper
2   Tbsp./30 mL olive oil
2   Tbsp./30 mL balsamic vinegar
½   tsp./2 mL grated lemon rind

Put onions in a large pan and cover with the wine and vinegar. Cook over low heat until the liquid is absorbed, about 30 minutes.

Add the water and cook for 30 minutes longer. Stir occasionally, being careful not to let the onions burn.

Add the honey and butter, stir, then season with salt and pepper to taste and set aside.

Season the fillets with salt and pepper to taste. In a medium-sized skillet, heat the oil over medium-high heat. When it is almost smoking, add the fillets and cook for about 3 minutes on each side until light brown. Set aside.

Add the balsamic vinegar to the onions and let warm for about 1 minute. Spoon the onions onto warm plates and arrange the fillets on top. Sprinkle with the lemon rind.

Serves 4.

Suggested Wine

Full-bodied white

Italy
Ruffino "Libaio" Chardonnay

United States (California)
Matanzas Creek Chardonnay

Australia
Penfolds "Koonunga Hill" Chardonnay

Fish and Seafood

Tonno aromatico
Tuna in a Fresh Herb Sauce

4	fillets of fresh tuna, 8 oz./250 g each	1	tsp./5 mL finely chopped
	salt		fresh chervil
	freshly ground black pepper	3	Tbsp./45 mL extra virgin olive oil
1	medium-sized firm, ripe tomato	1½	tsp./7 mL butter
1	tsp./5 mL finely chopped	½	shallot, finely chopped
	fresh thyme	½	clove garlic, finely chopped
1	tsp./5 mL finely chopped		juice from ½ lemon
	fresh tarragon	4	sprigs fresh parsley
1	tsp./5 mL finely chopped		
	fresh marjoram		

Rinse the tuna fillets under cold running water and pat dry with paper towels. Season with salt and pepper and set aside.

Remove the eye from the tomato and cut an x in the top. Blanch the tomato in a pot of boiling water for about 10 seconds, then plunge into a pot of cold water. Peel and cut into ½ inch/1.5 cm cubes. Mix the tomato cubes with the fresh herbs and 2 Tbsp./30 mL of the olive oil and set aside.

In a large skillet, melt the butter over medium heat. Add the shallot, garlic, remaining 1 Tbsp./15 mL of olive oil and the tuna fillets. Sauté both sides of the fish until golden brown, about 3–5 minutes each side. Remove from the skillet and arrange fillets on warm plates. Set aside.

In the same skillet, add the mixture of fresh herbs and tomato. Toss for a few seconds, until warm. Spoon the sauce over each tuna fillet and drizzle with lemon juice. Garnish with parsley sprigs.

Serves 4.

Suggested Wine

Medium- to full-bodied white

Italy
Ruffino Cabreo la Pietra

South Africa
Mulderbosch Sauvignon Blanc

France
Pierre Sparr Riesling Reserve

Scorfano del pescatore
Red Snapper in Lemon-Caper Sauce

4	fillets of fresh red snapper, 8 oz./250 g each
	salt
	freshly ground black pepper
2	medium-sized firm tomatoes
2	lemons, peeled
¼	cup/50 mL milk
1	cup/250 mL flour
2	Tbsp./30 mL olive oil
3	Tbsp./45 mL butter
1	spring onion, finely chopped
1	Tbsp./15 mL washed and coarsely chopped capers
1	Tbsp./15 mL finely chopped fresh parsley

Rinse the fillets under cold running water and pat dry with paper towels. Season with salt and pepper to taste and set aside.

Remove the eyes from the tomatoes and cut an x in the top of each. Blanch the tomatoes in a pot of boiling water for about 10 seconds, then plunge into a pot of cold water. Peel and cut into ½ inch/1.5 cm cubes. Set aside.

Cut the lemons into small cubes. Set aside.

Coat the fillets with the milk, then with the flour, shaking off any excess flour. In a large sauté pan, heat the olive oil. When it is hot, add the fillets and cook for 1 minute on each side over medium heat. Add 2 Tbsp./ 30 mL of the butter to the pan and let it foam. Remove the fish from the pan and put on a warm serving plate.

In the same pan, toss the spring onion and capers. Add the remaining 1 Tbsp./15 mL of butter, the lemon and tomato cubes and cook for 30 seconds. Spoon the sauce over the snapper and sprinkle with parsley.

Serves 4.

Suggested Wine

Medium-bodied white

Italy
Banfi Gavi Principessa

France
Jaffelin Bourgogne Aligoté

Australia
Tyrrell's Semillon-Sauvignon Blanc

Persico al pesto
Orange Roughy with Pesto

4	*fillets of fresh orange roughy, 6 oz./170 g each*		**Pesto**
	salt	4	*cloves garlic, peeled*
	freshly ground black pepper	½	*cup/125 mL fresh basil leaves*
		6	*Tbsp./90 mL olive oil*
			salt
			freshly ground black pepper
		2	*Tbsp./30 mL butter*
		1	*medium onion, sliced*
		6	*ripe tomatoes, seeded and diced*
		¼	*cup/50 mL apple cider or dry white wine*
		6	*fresh basil leaves, coarsely chopped*

Preheat the oven to 450°F/230°C.

Rinse the fillets under cold running water and pat dry with paper towels. Season with salt and pepper to taste and set aside.

To make the pesto sauce, place the garlic, basil, oil, and salt and pepper to taste in a blender and blend until thick and creamy. Remove from the blender and set aside.

In a heavy skillet over medium heat, melt the butter and cook the onion for 2 minutes, then add the tomatoes and cook another 2 minutes.

Place the roughy fillets on the bed of onion and tomatoes. Spoon the cider or wine and 1 tsp./5 mL of pesto onto each fillet.

Place the skillet in the preheated oven and bake for 8–10 minutes. Remove from the oven and arrange the fillets on a warm serving platter. Spoon the tomato and onion sauce from the pan around them. Garnish with the basil.

Serves 4.

Suggested Wine

Medium- to full-bodied white

Italy
Friulvini Tocai Grave del Friuli

New Zealand
Oyster Bay Sauvignon Blanc

France
Michel Redde Pouilly-Fumé

Baccalà con il pomodoro e prugne
Poached Cod with Tomatoes and Prunes

1/3   cup/75 mL olive oil
2   whole cloves garlic, peeled
1   cup/250 mL dry sherry
2   cups/500 mL canned imported
      Italian tomatoes with juice
      (put through a strainer or food
      mill to remove the seeds)
      salt
      freshly ground black pepper

4   fillets of fresh cod (about 2 lb./
      1 kg), 1 inch/2.5 cm thick
1/2   cup/125 mL pitted prunes, diced
3   Tbsp./45 mL finely chopped
      fresh parsley

Heat the oil in a large skillet over medium heat. Add the garlic and cook, stirring occasionally, until it is golden brown on all sides. Discard the garlic and add the sherry. Cook until the sherry is reduced by half, about 3–4 minutes. Add the strained tomatoes, season with salt and pepper to taste and bring to a boil. Lower the heat to medium and add the cod. Cover the skillet, leaving the cover slightly askew. Cook the cod for 10–12 minutes, until it is tender and flaky (pierce with a fork to test). Gently place the fish on serving dishes and keep warm in a low oven while you finish the sauce.

Add the prunes and parsley to the sauce and simmer 2–3 minutes. Spoon the sauce over the fish and serve.

Serves 4.

^ Suggested Wine

Medium-bodied fruity white

Italy
Hofstätter Pinot Bianco

United States (Washington)
Hogue Cellars Johannisberg Riesling

France
Hugel Sylvaner "Hugel"

> Suggested Wine

Fruity, medium-bodied white

Italy
Castello Banfi Pinot Grigio "Le Rime"

New Zealand
Nobilo White Cloud

Canada (British Columbia)
Mission Hill Gewürztraminer Grand Reserve

Salmone al cartoccio viareggio
Salmon in Papillote with Lime

2   fillets of fresh salmon,
      6–8 oz./170–250 g each
      salt
      white pepper
2   leeks, white part only, julienned
2   carrots, julienned
2   stalks celery, julienned
      pinch grated ginger root
2   medium shallots, minced
2   tsp./10 mL lime zest
2   Tbsp./30 mL butter
2   Tbsp./30 mL olive oil
2   Tbsp./30 mL dry white wine
      juice of 1 lime
2   tsp./10 mL finely chopped
      fresh parsley

Preheat the oven to 400°F/200°C.

Butter two 12 inch/30 cm squares of aluminum foil. Arrange a salmon fillet on each square and season the fish with salt and pepper. Sprinkle the julienned vegetables over the fish. Add the ginger, shallots and lime zest.

In a small bowl, mix the butter, oil, wine and lime juice. Pour over the salmon fillets. Wrap the foil around the fish like an envelope. Place the two foil packets on a baking tray and cook in the preheated oven for approximately 12–15 minutes.

Remove the tray from the oven. Serve the salmon in the foil. Garnish with parsley.

Serves 2.

Fish and Seafood

Luccio al rosmarino
Pike in Rosemary Sauce

1½ lb./750 g fillets of fresh pike,
* bones removed*
1¼ cups/300 mL fish stock
* (see recipe, p. 146)*
6   sprigs fresh rosemary
¾ cup/175 mL whipping cream
1½ tsp./7 mL butter
2   Tbsp./30 mL olive oil

Rinse the pike fillets under cold running water and pat dry with paper towels. Set aside.

Put the fish stock and 2 of the rosemary sprigs in a pot and simmer over medium heat until reduced by half. Add the cream to the pot and remove the rosemary sprigs. Continue simmering until the sauce is slightly thickened and creamy. Set aside and keep warm.

In a large skillet, melt the butter, then add the oil. When it is hot, brown the pike fillets on both sides over medium heat for 3 minutes. Remove the fillets from the skillet and keep warm.

Add the rosemary sauce to the skillet and heat just to the boiling point. Coat four warm plates with the sauce and place a pike fillet on each. Garnish with the remaining 4 rosemary sprigs. Serve small boiled potatoes on the side.

Serves 4.

Baccalà in umido
Braised Salt Cod with Tomatoes, Black Olives and Silver Onions

1½ lb./750 g fillet of dried salt cod
1½ cups/375 mL silver onions
¼ cup/50 mL olive oil
2   28 oz./796 mL cans of peeled
* Italian plum tomatoes, drained*
* and crushed*
½ tsp./2 mL finely chopped garlic
2   tsp./10 mL finely chopped
* fresh parsley*
1   tsp./5 mL finely chopped
* fresh basil*

½ tsp./2 mL finely chopped
* fresh rosemary*
½ tsp./2 mL finely chopped
* fresh oregano*
½ tsp./2 mL finely chopped
* fresh thyme*
* freshly ground black pepper*
¼ cup/50 mL pitted and sliced
* Calamata black olives*

Soak the cod in a pan of cold water for 12–24 hours, depending on the saltiness of the cure. Drain off the water and cut the cod into 2 inch/5 cm cubes. Return the fish to the pan and cover with water. Bring the water to a boil on top of the stove and skim. Reduce the heat and poach the cod for approximately 15 minutes, then drain and set aside.

In a large pot, sauté the onions in the oil for 3–5 minutes. Add the tomatoes, garlic and parsley and mix together. Season with the basil, rosemary, oregano, thyme and pepper to taste. Add the cod and bring the contents of the pot to a boil. Reduce the heat, cover and cook for approximately 15 minutes, until the fish is tender. Add the olives, replace the cover and cook for an additional 2 minutes. Check the seasoning and adjust, if necessary. Transfer the contents of the pot to a platter or individual plates and serve immediately.

Serves 4.

< Suggested Wine

Medium-bodied white

Italy
Zenato Lugana

France
Labouré-Roi Domaine des Courtelongs
Mâcon-Villages

United States (California)
Pine Ridge Chenin Blanc

^ Suggested Wine

Medium- to full-bodied white

Italy
Zenato Lugana

Portugal
Caves Aliança Bairrada Reserva

Spain
Torres Viña Sol

Filetti di spigola olio e limone
Poached Fillet of Sea Bass with Olive Oil and Lemon

4	fillets of fresh sea bass, 6–8 oz./ 170–250 g each
	salt
	freshly ground black pepper
	juice of 1 lemon
¼	tsp./1 mL finely chopped garlic
¼	tsp./1 mL peeled and finely chopped fresh ginger root
2	Tbsp./30 mL finely chopped fresh cilantro
2	Tbsp./30 mL extra virgin olive oil
	juice of 1 lemon
4	tsp./20 mL extra virgin olive oil
12	sprigs fresh cilantro
4	slices lemon
½	cup/125 mL chicken stock (see recipe, p. 147)
4	tsp./20 mL extra virgin olive oil
4	sprigs fresh cilantro
1	lemon, cut into 4 wedges

Rinse the fillets of sea bass under cold running water and pat dry with paper towels. Season with salt and pepper and put in a buttered baking pan. Sprinkle with the lemon juice, garlic, ginger and cilantro. Drizzle with the olive oil and refrigerate for 30 minutes, then remove the pan from the refrigerator.

Preheat the oven to 375°F/190°C.

Sprinkle the sea bass with the lemon juice and drizzle each fillet with 1 tsp./5 mL of the olive oil. Put 3 sprigs of cilantro and 1 slice of lemon on top of each fillet.

Add the chicken stock to the baking pan and bring to a boil on top of the stove. Cover the pan with a sheet of buttered foil. Put the pan in the preheated oven and poach the fish for 8–12 minutes, then remove the pan from the oven and transfer the fillets to a warm platter or individual plates.

Drizzle each fillet with 1 tsp./5 mL of olive oil and put a fresh sprig of cilantro on top of each. Garnish the platter or plates with lemon wedges and serve immediately.

Serves 4.

Suggested Wine

Medium-bodied white

Italy
Antinori Orvieto Classico

Canada (British Columbia)
Gray Monk Pinot Blanc

Australia
Lindeman's Semillon-Chardonnay "Bin 77"

Crostata di gamberetti e zucchini
Shrimp and Zucchini Tart

Pie Crust

2	cups/500 mL flour
½	tsp./2 mL salt
¼	tsp./1 mL baking powder
2	Tbsp./30 mL sugar
¾	cup/175 mL butter
½	cup/125 mL ice-cold water

Filling

1	medium zucchini, washed and julienned
1	Tbsp./15 mL olive oil
½	lb./250 g fresh shrimp, cleaned
¼	tsp./1 mL fresh thyme
	salt
	freshly ground black pepper
2	large eggs
1	cup/250 mL whipping cream
	pinch ground nutmeg
¼	cup/50 mL freshly grated Fontina cheese
¼	cup/50 mL freshly grated Gruyère cheese
¼	cup/50 mL freshly grated mozzarella cheese

Preheat the oven to 350°F/180°C.

To make the pie crust, mix the flour, salt, baking powder and sugar in a bowl. Using a pastry blender, cut the butter into the flour mixture and mix until crumbly. Add the water, a little at a time, using just enough water to bind the mixture, until a dough is formed. Roll the dough into a ball, handling as little as possible. With a rolling pin, roll out the dough to an even thickness of ¼ inch/5 mm.

Butter the bottom of a 9 inch/23 cm pie plate and lightly dust with flour. Put the dough into the pie plate and gently press it to the shape of the plate using your fingertips. Prick the dough with a fork in several places. Put in the preheated oven and pre-bake the pie shell for approximately 8 minutes, until lightly golden. Remove from the oven and set aside. (Do not turn off the oven.)

In a small skillet, sauté the zucchini in the oil 2–3 minutes, until soft. Fill the bottom of the pie shell with the zucchini and shrimp. Season with the thyme and salt and pepper to taste. Set aside.

Beat the eggs and cream together in a bowl. Season with the nutmeg. Pour this mixture over the zucchini and shrimp and set aside. Mix the three cheeses together in a bowl. Sprinkle over the egg mixture.

Put the pie plate in the preheated oven and bake for 20–25 minutes, until the filling is firm. Remove from the oven and allow the pie to sit for approximately 10 minutes before serving. Cut into wedges and serve on individual plates with a crisp green salad on the side.

Serves 8.

Suggested Wine

Light- to medium-bodied white

Italy
Hofstätter Pinot Bianco

France
Pierre Sparr Chasselas Vieilles Vignes

Canada (British Columbia)
Gray Monk Pinot Auxerrois

Fish and Seafood

> Sole and Salmon Roulade with Saffron, *page 88*

Filetti di sogliola e scampi con taccole
Sole and Scampi with Snow Peas

½	lb./250 g snow peas
6	Tbsp./90 mL butter
1	medium shallot, finely chopped
⅔	cup/150 mL fish stock (see recipe, p. 146)
¾	cup/175 mL dry red wine
1	tsp./5 mL sugar

16	medium scampi, peeled
12	fresh fillets of sole
¼	cup/50 mL fish stock
	salt
	freshly ground black pepper
1	Tbsp./15 mL finely chopped fresh parsley

Preheat the oven to 400°F/200°C.

Clean and wash the snow peas. Boil them in salted water for 2 minutes, until cooked but still firm. Drain and cool under cold running water. Pat dry with a paper towel and set aside.

In a small saucepan, melt 2 Tbsp./30 mL of the butter, add the shallot and cook over medium heat until the shallot is transparent. Add ⅔ cup/150 mL of fish stock, wine and sugar and simmer over low heat until reduced to three-quarters. Set aside.

Rinse the scampi and the sole fillets under cold running water, drain and pat dry with paper towels. Butter the bottom of a baking dish and arrange the fillets in the dish. Drizzle with ¼ cup/50 mL fish stock and bake in the preheated oven for 2 minutes. Add the scampi and cook for 1 more minute. Remove the baking dish from the oven.

Pour the liquid from the dish into a saucepan. Add the wine and fish stock mixture and 3 Tbsp./45 mL of the butter and whisk over high heat. Season to taste with salt and pepper.

Rewarm the snow peas in a medium skillet with the remaining 1 Tbsp./15 mL of butter. Arrange them on warm plates and top with the scampi and sole. Spoon the sauce over and sprinkle with the parsley.

Serves 4.

Suggested Wine

Light- to medium-bodied white or sparkling

Italy
Mezza Corona Pinot Grigio "Trentino" (white)

South Africa
Libertas Chenin Blanc (white)

Spain
Segura Viudas Brut Reserva (sparkling)

Involtini di sogliola e salmone zafferanati
Sole and Salmon Roulade with Saffron

2	fillets of fresh sole, 4 oz./115 g each
1	fillet of fresh salmon, 4 oz./115 g, thinly sliced
	salt
	white pepper
1	tsp./5 mL chopped fresh dill
1	tsp./5 mL grated fresh horseradish
1	green onion, sliced
	zest of 1 orange
	zest of ½ lemon
1	Tbsp./15 mL flour
2	Tbsp./30 mL butter
½	cup/125 mL dry white wine
	pinch saffron threads
1	Tbsp./15 mL dry white wine
	juice of ½ lemon
1	Tbsp./15 mL butter

Preheat the oven to 400°F/200°C.

Rinse the sole and salmon fillets under cold running water and pat dry with paper towels. Season with salt and pepper. Place the sole fillets skin side up on a flat surface and lay the salmon slices on top of them. Sprinkle the salmon with the dill, horseradish, green onion and orange and lemon zest. Fold each sole fillet to make a square. Bring the sides of the folded fillets together, overlapping them at the centre. Dust the fish rolls with the flour.

In a medium-sized ovenproof skillet, melt the butter over medium heat and add the fish, folded side down. Let the fillets brown for 2 minutes, then, using a rubber spatula, turn the rolls gently and brown the other side for 2 minutes. Turn the fish rolls so that the folded side is down. Remove from the heat.

Mix the wine and saffron together and pour over the fish. Place the skillet in the preheated oven and bake for 8–10 minutes. Remove the fish to a serving platter and keep warm.

Place the skillet over medium heat and combine the wine, lemon juice and butter. Adjust the seasoning. Simmer until the sauce is velvety. Strain the sauce through a sieve over the fish rolls. Serve with parsleyed new potatoes, peeled and steamed, and braised leeks.

Serves 2.

Suggested Wine

Crisp, medium-bodied white

Italy
Pietrafitta Vernaccia di San Gimignano

Chile
Caliterra Sauvignon Blanc

United States (Washington)
Columbia Winery Semillon

Salmone fresco marinato
Salmon Gravlox Marinated with Dill

2	*fillets of fresh salmon, 1 lb./500 g each, skin off*		1	*Tbsp./15 mL dry gin*
2	*Tbsp./30 mL coarse salt*		2	*Tbsp./30 mL olive oil*
1	*Tbsp./15 mL cracked white peppercorns*		1	*bunch fresh dill*
			8	*sprigs fresh dill*
2	*Tbsp./30 mL sugar*		2	*lemons, cut into 8 wedges*

Rinse the salmon fillets under cold running water and pat dry with a paper towel. Set aside.

Mix the salt, peppercorns and sugar in a bowl. Rub this seasoning mixture into the salmon. Then rub the salmon fillets with the gin and olive oil. Put 1 fillet in a baking dish and cover the top with fresh dill. Place the other fillet on top of the first. Place a wooden board over both fillets and top with a 5–10 lb./2.5–5 kg weight. Store the salmon in the refrigerator and allow it to marinate in the gin and dill for 48 hours. Turn the fillets over approximately every 6 hours.

Remove the baking dish from the refrigerator. Remove the weight and wooden board and place the fillets on a cutting board. Cut the salmon into 8 thin slices and place on a platter. Garnish each slice of salmon with 1 sprig of dill and garnish the platter with lemon wedges.

Serves 8.

Note: Leftover salmon may be frozen and served again.

Suggested Wine

Crisp, dry, medium-bodied white

Italy
Teruzzi & Puthod Terre di Tufi

France
Barton & Guestier 1725 Blanc

Australia
Lindeman's Sauvignon Blanc "Bin 95"

Calamari ripieni
Stuffed Calamari

2	lb./1 kg squid			salt
				freshly ground black pepper
	Stuffing		1	egg
1	Tbsp./15 mL olive oil		¼	cup/50 mL fine bread crumbs, dry or fresh
3	oz./90 g prosciutto			rind of 1 lemon, grated
1	small onion, finely chopped			
2	cloves garlic, finely chopped		2	Tbsp./30 mL olive oil
1	Tbsp./15 mL finely chopped fresh parsley		2	Tbsp./30 mL butter
2	tsp./10 mL finely chopped fresh lemon thyme		½	cup/125 mL dry white wine fresh parsley, finely chopped
1	tsp./5 mL finely chopped fresh oregano			

Preheat the oven to 350°F/180°C.

Clean the squid by pulling off the head and pulling out the entrails. Cut off the tentacles, making sure to discard the beaklike mouth. Chop the tentacles and reserve for the stuffing.

To prepare the stuffing, heat the oil in a medium-sized sauté pan and cook the squid tentacles, prosciutto, onion, garlic and herbs over medium heat for 2–3 minutes. Season with salt and pepper to taste. Remove from the heat and transfer the mixture to a bowl. Add the egg, bread crumbs and grated lemon rind and mix until the texture of the stuffing is smooth. Using a piping bag, fill the squid tubes with the stuffing and seal each end with a toothpick. Season the squid with salt and pepper. Put the oil and butter in a medium-sized ovenproof skillet and brown the squid over medium heat for 3–4 minutes on each side.

Place the skillet in the preheated oven for 8 minutes. Remove the pan from the oven, pour off the grease and add the wine.

Serve the squid whole or sliced in four even pieces. Pour the pan sauce over and around the squid. Garnish with parsley.

This recipe is best served on a bed of steamed rice.

Serves 4.

Suggested Wine

Medium- to full-bodied white

Italy
Antinori Cervaro della Sala

United States (New York)
Palmer Chardonnay

New Zealand
Vavasour Chardonnay Reserve

Ostriche alla fiorentina
Oysters Florentine

2	bunches fresh spinach
1	Tbsp./15 mL finely chopped onion
2	Tbsp./30 mL butter
¼	cup/50 mL white sauce (see recipe, p. 145)
	pinch nutmeg
	salt
	freshly ground black pepper
12	fresh oysters in the shell or 12 oz./340 g shucked oysters
¼	cup/50 mL coarsely grated Parmesan cheese
1	lemon, cut into wedges
2	sprigs fresh parsley

Preheat the oven to 400°F/200°C.

Wash and stem the spinach. Discard any limp or discoloured leaves. Blanch the spinach by dropping it into a saucepan of boiling water, then drain. Finely chop the spinach and set aside.

Sauté the onion in butter in a skillet over medium heat until transparent, then add to the spinach. Add the white sauce and mix thoroughly. Season the mixture with the nutmeg and salt and pepper to taste.

Put a small amount of the spinach mixture on the deepest side of each oyster shell and put an oyster on top of each filled shell. (If using shucked oysters, place them in ovenproof dishes.) Coat the oyster/spinach mixture with a small amount of the white sauce. Sprinkle the Parmesan cheese on top. Place the oysters on a baking sheet and put in the preheated oven. Bake for 15 minutes, then put under the broiler for 2–3 minutes, until the cheese turns brown.

Serve the oysters in the shell on a bed of rock salt to keep them steady. Garnish with lemon wedges and sprigs of parsley.

Serves 2.

Suggested Wine

Medium-bodied white

Italy
Zenato Lugana

France
Henri Bourgeois Sancerre Blanc "Les Baronnes"

United States (Washington)
Château Ste. Michelle Sauvignon Blanc

Spiedino di salmone e gambero
Prawn and Salmon Kebabs with Mint Sauce

20	large prawns
½	lb./250 g fillets of fresh salmon
	salt
	freshly ground black pepper

Mint Sauce

7	Tbsp./100 mL prawn butter (see recipe, p. 149)
4	fresh mint leaves, chopped
¼	cup/50 mL fish stock (see recipe, p. 146)
⅓	cup + 1 Tbsp./100 mL whipping cream
1	Tbsp./15 mL butter
2	Tbsp./30 mL olive oil
	juice from ½ lemon
1	Tbsp./15 mL finely chopped fresh parsley

Boil the prawns in salted water for approximately 1 minute. Drain and cool under cold running water. Peel and devein the prawns, then set aside.

Cut the salmon into 20 cubes, ¾ inch/2 cm thick. Season the salmon with salt and pepper to taste and set aside.

Skewer the prawns and salmon cubes alternately on 8 kebabs.

To make the mint sauce, melt the prawn butter in a small saucepan, then add the mint leaves and fish stock and cook until reduced by half.

Add the cream and reduce by half, simmering for 10 minutes. Set aside and keep warm.

Heat the butter and oil in a large skillet over medium heat. Add the salmon and prawn kebabs and cook for 2 minutes on each side, until the salmon is lightly browned.

Serve the kebabs on warm plates. Spoon the mint sauce over, drizzle with lemon juice and sprinkle with parsley.

Serves 4.

Suggested Wine

Light- to medium-bodied white

Italy
Collavini Chardonnay Grave del Friuli

United States (California)
Raymond Napa Valley Sauvignon Blanc

France
Rothschild Mouton Cadet Blanc

Capesante con burro di rapa
Pan-Fried Scallops with Horseradish Butter

1½ lb./750 g fresh scallops
  salt
  white pepper
  juice of 1 lemon
  flour for dredging
⅓ cup/75 mL vegetable oil
  horseradish butter

Horseradish Butter
5 Tbsp./75 mL butter, at room temperature
4 tsp./20 mL prepared horseradish juice of ½ lemon
3 drops Worcestershire sauce
1 Tbsp./15 mL dry white wine
4 tsp./20 mL finely chopped fresh parsley
  salt
  white pepper

Rinse the scallops under cold running water and set aside to drain. Season with salt and pepper. Sprinkle with lemon juice and dust with flour.

Heat the oil in a skillet over medium-high heat and fry the scallops for 3–4 minutes per side, until slightly brown, then remove from the skillet and put on individual plates. Top each serving with 4 tsp./20 mL horseradish butter. Serve with long-grain white rice.

Serves 4.

Put the butter, horseradish, lemon juice, Worcestershire sauce, wine, parsley, and salt and pepper to taste in a mixing bowl and whip for approximately 10 minutes, until the butter triples in volume. Make the horseradish butter in advance and store in the refrigerator until ready to use.

Note: Leftover horseradish butter may be frozen for later use.

Suggested Wine

Medium-bodied white

Italy
Bolla Soave Classico "Castellaro"

South Africa
Kleindal Sauvignon Blanc

United States (California)
Vendange Sauvignon Blanc

Meat, Fowl, Game

Italians still eat a fair amount of meat. Most beef has to be imported, for Italy has a mountainous terrain and cannot sustain substantial cattle grazing, so veal and beef are considered luxuries outside rural farming areas.

Fowl, especially chicken, which is readily available from any market, is perhaps the most widely served dish in Italy. I could happily eat chicken every day of the week and have striven to make myself an expert on its qualities. When purchasing a chicken, I want to know how it was raised, what it was fed and something about its fat content. It's a good idea to get to know your butcher and ask such questions, whether you are looking for a fryer, roaster or stewing chicken. In any case, you will want as lean a bird as possible, and preferably one that is free-range.

It's hard to imagine anyone who has not had occasion to cook a chicken. The meat is so mild and tender that it lends itself to the simplest as well as the most extravagant

< Veal Stew with Artichokes and Peas, *page 103*

of culinary treatments. There may not be enough paper in the world to accommodate all the chicken recipes. My favourite, of course, is Mamma's crispy and juicy roasted chicken—a most elegant way to serve a bird.

Which reminds me of my "Holy Chicken" story. When I was around ten years old, I served as an altar boy at the 11:00 A.M. mass of our local church. It was a great privilege to be chosen for this role, and my mother was beside herself with joy. On Sundays, food was prepared and served after the late morning mass. People would dress in their best clothes, bells would ring out, and everyone would be proud to be part of a special occasion.

As in most churches, the priest's residence was located behind the altar. When the housekeeper was preparing Sunday's lunch, the aroma of roast chicken rubbed with oregano and rosemary would drift through the open doors and over the altar. These delicious smells always seemed to find their way directly to my nose.

One Sunday after months of such torture I saw the housekeeper come into the church to receive communion. As the priest was distributing Holy Communion, I made a quick trip to the kitchen. When I saw the golden brown bird, I said, "Sorry, God, I just have to have a crispy leg," and broke one off and stuffed it into my mouth. Then, just as quickly, I returned to my duties at the altar. That evening at the five o'clock mass, a one-legged chicken was the feature of the priest's sermon.

The following Sunday as I took

confession, I unburdened myself of my sin by confessing that I had been the culprit who removed the chicken leg. For penance, the priest gave me five "Our Father's" and twenty-five "Hail Mary's" to say after mass. But my penance was doubled because while I was saying my prayers, everyone else was eating roast chicken for lunch and there was none left over for me. I do feel that I am now entitled to eat all the chicken I want, as I have prayed enough.

Many years later, I drove to Whistler ski resort to visit a friend who had rented a cabin there. Upon locating the address, I rang the bell, but no one answered. The door was unlocked, so I took the liberty of letting myself in and called out a greeting. I could hear someone in the shower, so while I waited for my friend to appear, I checked the oven (a habit of chefs) and found a skinny, pale-looking chicken sitting there forlornly. Deciding to be helpful, I poked around the cupboards and found some pine nuts, some green olives, some onion. I was gleefully adding these savory ingredients to the chicken when I heard a scream. Turning around, I saw a total stranger, and it struck me that this must not be 2215 Mountain Road after all. Before the man could call the police, I hastily explained that I had obviously wandered into the wrong cabin, that I was in the restaurant business and that I had impulsively spiced up his chicken. At that point, seeing that the bird was looking interesting, he asked me for the name of the recipe. My off-the-cuff answer was "Happy Chicken." He later wrote me a thank-you note and requested a copy of the recipe for a chicken he had thoroughly enjoyed.

Turkey is the other bird that appears quite often on our tables in Italy. When I was young, our family used to eat turkey once a week, served not as a whole bird but as a fillet rolled and stuffed with vegetables, or breaded. At Christmas, Easter or harvest time, turkey is cooked whole. Other birds associated with festive occasions include goose, duck and pheasant. Wild birds such as quail, partridge, pigeon and squab start to appear on country tables at the opening of the fall hunting season. Then, beginning early in the morning, you can hear a steady "pop, pop, pop," and it seems as if all of Italy is in the countryside shooting off guns. Wild boar, hare and venison are also fall and winter dishes served in restaurants and at home during the hunting season. Over the years, I have maintained a tradition of serving a leg of venison every Christmas—a festive presentation for my family and for friends who otherwise might not have an opportunity to experience this dish. In this book, I have included classic game dishes that call for game available in North American markets, not just in Italy.

Italians are recognized the world over for their veal dishes, although veal is equally popular on the menus of other countries. It is true, though, that Italians were the first to feature veal as a main dish, and it has always been more popular in Italy than beef. I think the reason for this is that veal was home raised and calves required less space than beeves, being milk fed rather than grass fed. Veal is also often preferred in home cooking in the preparation of meat sauces because it brings a lighter texture and less fat to the dish. Italians have always enjoyed their veal prepared in the simplest ways, most often grilled or roasted. And, of course, we are all familiar with veal scaloppine in a white wine sauce.

As a Tuscan, I was first introduced to *vitellone* (a large, grass-fed veal) from the Valdichiana region of central Italy. The best-known veal dish of the region is called *Bistecca alla fiorentina*, a famous dish in Florence. (In North America, this term refers to a Porterhouse or T-bone steak.) Usually cooked over a wood charcoal grill, the meat is drizzled with olive oil and seasoned with salt and pepper.

Later, as I travelled outside Italy, I discovered that in Europe beef is more popular than veal. My true love for beef developed when I was working in England. I was spending my first Christmas away from home, and as the festive spirit of the season grew and the shop decorations, the music and the colourful lights appeared, I became more and more depressed. Here I was in a cold northern climate far from my warm Mediterranean home, my family and friends. Then a young lady I had met on the Isle of Jersey came to my rescue. She invited me to spend Christmas with her and her family, and I quickly accepted. The Christmas dinner roast of beef was one of the juiciest I have ever tasted—crispy on the outside and ranging from pink to well done on the inside, running with clear juices. It was accompanied by a puffy Yorkshire pudding, petit pois with melted butter, mashed potatoes and the silkiest of gravies. I recall the host, Mr. Blackwood, a British banker and a golfer, observing me accept a fourth helping and asking: "My goodness, when was the last time you ate?" His second question was: "Do Italians like roast beef?" And the third: "What are your intentions with my daughter?" After a moment of silence, I replied to all three questions: "Thank you very much, I like English people."

This was one of the warmest, most memorable meals I can remember. If you ever want to invite me to dinner, just serve me very thinly sliced roast beef, green peas and mashed potatoes. It's fine if you don't want to prepare a Yorkshire pudding.

In North America, more beef is consumed than any other type of meat. Always look for the leanest cuts, and when dining out, select those prepared with as little sauce as possible. This will allow you to more fully enjoy the taste and texture of the meat.

Pork is another locally raised meat in Italy and is traditionally the most widely consumed meat in a family setting. Besides roast pork, it takes the form of sausage, prosciutto and ground meat for ragus.

Our family always kept four or five pigs, and as a young man it was my responsibility to look after these animals until they were ready for consumption. I also participated in the

making of sausages, prosciutto, salami, bacon loins and ribs, which kept us well supplied over the winter. Everything between the nose and the tail was used at home. In the markets we sometimes saw a whole roasted suckling pig that would be thinly sliced for sandwiches. Which reminds me of a story.

One weekend several years ago, I was invited to my friend David McLean's cottage on Bowen Island. My contribution was to bring enough meat for sixteen people. Because it was a long weekend, my local market was already sold out of everything interesting. Then I had the bright idea of phoning a farmer in the Fraser Valley and ordering a small pig. I took for granted that he would know I needed a butchered piglet, or one at least dressed for the party. When I arrived at his farm the next morning, I was presented with a choice of twenty very live pigs. I picked the smallest one and took it along for the ride. Getting the live pig into my car was a major event (memories of my childhood came flooding back), and reaching the cottage by ferry is a story by itself. You can imagine the surprise of my host as I unloaded dinner. Since there was enough food for the first day, we reserved preparing the piglet until day two.

We kept our wiggling friend tied to a tree, where he was continuously fed by the guests, and so by the second day had already gained two pounds. He was even given a bath with hot, soapy water and nicknamed Paul Newman because of his brilliant blue eyes.

I stayed awake all night worrying about how I would handle the job of butchering, but when I went outside next morning, I discovered that the ladies had let "Paul" loose in the forest. Secretly, I was relieved and told everyone I didn't think I had the courage to go through with the deed. They all approved, and we then joined in the search for little blue eyes so that I could return him to the farm.

I received many invitations to the McLeans' over the years thereafter, but they specifically requested that I not bring any food.

I do have some interesting pork recipes in this book that don't involve a trip to the farm. Lean pork is readily available in our markets, it is very low in cholesterol, and there is a variety of cuts to choose from.

I mentioned earlier that Tuscans are crazy hunters. My only North American hunting experience took place north of Chilko Lake in British Columbia's Chilcotin region, with two restaurateur friends, Jean-Claude Ramond and Jean-Paul Pratolini. Alan Daniels of the *Vancouver Sun* has written graphically about this episode:

The last time three suspicious-looking foreigners opened a crate of lobster mayonnaise and uncorked a bottle of Beaujolais Village and proceeded to eat breakfast at Williams Lake airport at 10:30 in the morning, the incident provoked understandable confusion among those who witnessed it.

The three foreigners claimed they were hunters, which was obviously ridiculous. And as their baggage was unloaded from the light plane that had ferried them from Vancouver, it appeared that they had come not only for breakfast, but for lunch and dinner too.

They had brought 40 loaves of Italian bread, four legs of lamb, a rack of lamb, two New York strips (enough for 16 steaks), three cases of Beaune, five cases of Champdeville, a case of Blanc de Blanc, Martin and Martini Rossi, some vodka, some Iranian caviar, the aforementioned lobster, assorted cold cuts, spices, pots, pans, plates, glasses and a carton of Monte Cristo cigars.

They also had a rifle, each, and about 15 pounds of ammunition, with which, presumably, they could defend themselves from marauding legs of lamb.

"When we go to the bush, we get hungry," they told anyone who would listen. "Why eat a hamburger, when with a little planning, we can eat pepper steak, or terrine. We like to eat well, so we bring our own food." It transpired they had come for a week.

Umberto is Italian, his friends are French and before they came to Canada none of them had ever been hunting. (This is probably providential, at least in Umberto's case. A few years ago it was reported in the world's press that 43 hunters were killed on the opening day of the Italian hunting season.) In any event, if past performances can be relied on, the big game of the Chilcotin would appear to be in little immediate danger.

"I've never killed nothing," confesses Umberto with disarming candor. "I'll tell you what kind of a hunter I am. A few days ago I went fishing and lost my cowboy hat. That's what kind of a hunter I am."

So if in the future you decide to go hunting, I would suggest that you be prepared to come home and look up a well-stocked supplier. There is really no need to hunt in the wild for your food anymore. Game today is as close as your butcher.

Arrosto di vitello con salsa di funghi
Roast Loin of Veal with Mushroom Sauce

3	lb./1.5 kg veal loin roast
	olive oil
	salt
	freshly ground black pepper
1	clove garlic, cut into slivers

Mushroom Sauce

1	tsp./5 mL olive oil
1	tsp./5 mL butter
1	cup/250 mL thinly sliced mushrooms
1/4	cup/50 mL dry white wine
1	cup/250 mL whipping cream
	salt
	freshly ground black pepper
2	tsp./10 mL finely chopped fresh parsley

Preheat the oven to 450°F/230°C.

Rub the veal with the oil and season with salt and pepper. Using the point of a sharp knife, make small incisions in the surface of the meat and insert the slivers of garlic into the incisions.

Put the veal in a shallow roasting pan and place in the preheated oven. Roast for 10 minutes, then reduce the heat to 350°F/180°C and continue cooking for 1 hour (20 minutes per pound/40 minutes per kilogram).

To make the sauce, sauté the mushrooms in the oil and butter in a skillet over medium heat for 3 minutes, until they are brown. Add the wine and the roasting pan juices to the mushrooms and stir until well blended. Add the cream to the mushrooms, stir until well blended and reduce by simmering over medium heat until the sauce thickens slightly. Season with salt and pepper to taste.

Carve the veal into ½ inch/1.5 cm thick slices. Serve on warm plates. Spoon the sauce over and sprinkle with the parsley.

Serves 6.

Suggested Wine

Medium- to full-bodied red

Italy
Ruffino Chianti Classico Riserva Ducale Gold Label

United States (California)
Saintsbury Pinot Noir Reserve

United States (Oregon)
Firesteed Pinot Noir

Osso buco
Braised Veal Shank

6   meaty veal shin bones
    salt
    freshly ground black pepper
¼   cup/50 mL flour
¼   cup/50 mL olive or vegetable oil

Sauce
1   large onion, finely chopped
1   tsp./5 mL olive oil
1   tsp./5 mL butter
1   medium carrot, finely chopped
1   stalk celery, finely chopped
2   cloves garlic, finely chopped
1   cup/250 mL dry red wine

28   oz./796 mL can of peeled Italian tomatoes, finely chopped, and their liquid (or equivalent amount of fresh tomatoes)
1   tsp./5 mL brown sugar
    salt
    freshly ground black pepper

Gremolata
2   tsp./10 mL grated lemon peel
1   clove garlic, finely chopped
4   tsp./20 mL finely chopped fresh parsley

Preheat the oven to 350°F/180°C.

Season the veal with salt and pepper to taste. Dip it in the flour, shaking off the excess. Heat the oil in a large skillet. Over medium heat, sauté the veal on all sides until brown to seal in the juices. Transfer the veal to a casserole dish just big enough to contain it.

To make the sauce, in a separate skillet, sauté the onion in the oil and butter over medium heat until the onion is transparent. Add the carrot, celery and garlic and sauté for 5 minutes. Add the wine, the tomatoes with their liquid and the brown sugar and stir until well blended. Season with salt and pepper to taste.

Pour the sauce over the veal and place the casserole dish, covered, in the preheated oven for 1½ hours. Uncover the casserole for the last 30 minutes.

To make the gremolata, mix the lemon peel, garlic and parsley in a bowl.

Serve the veal on a warm serving platter or on warm plates, sprinkled with gremolata.

Serves 6.

^ Suggested Wine
Full-bodied red

Italy
Produttori del Barbaresco Barbaresco "Ovello" Riserva
Tenuto Il Poggione Brunello di Montalcino

Spain
Torres Gran Coronas Black Label Reserva

> Suggested Wine
Medium-bodied red

Italy
Frescobaldi Rosso di Montalcino

Chile
Cousiño Macul Cabernet Sauvignon Antiguas Reservas

Hungary
Egervin Egri Bikaver

Costolette alla valdostana
Veal Chops Valdostana Style

4   large veal chops
4   oz./115 g Fontina cheese
4   slices prosciutto
    salt
    freshly ground black pepper
½   cup/125 mL all-purpose flour
3   eggs, beaten
1   tsp./5 mL finely chopped fresh parsley
½   cup/125 mL fine bread crumbs
¼   cup/50 mL butter

Make a horizontal slit in each chop to form a pocket for the filling. Cut the cheese into thin strips. Lay an equal number of cheese strips on each of the 4 prosciutto slices and roll up, flattening slightly. Insert one roll into each of the veal chop pockets, pounding the edges of the meat to close.

Season each chop on both sides with salt and pepper. Dip chops first into the flour, then the egg, then the parsley and bread crumbs.

Melt the butter in a large skillet and cook the chops over medium heat for about 20 minutes, turning frequently, until golden brown on both sides. Serve hot.

Serves 4.

Spezzatino di vitello con fricassea di carciofi e piselli
Veal Stew with Artichokes and Peas

1½ lb./750 g veal leg or loin, cut into
    1 inch/2.5 cm cubes
    salt
    freshly ground black pepper
4   small fresh artichokes, trimmed
    and quartered
¼   cup/50 mL olive oil
2   shallots, minced

3   Tbsp./45 mL butter
1   cup/250 mL fresh or frozen peas
⅔   cup/150 mL dry white wine
6   Tbsp./90 mL butter
    salt
    freshly ground black pepper
1   tsp./5 mL finely chopped
    fresh parsley

Season the veal with salt and pepper and set aside.

Blanch the artichokes in a pot of boiling salted water for 5 minutes. Remove from the pot and cool under cold running water.

Heat the oil over high heat in a large heavy-bottomed skillet. When the oil is hot, brown the veal cubes for approximately 4 minutes, stirring frequently. Add the shallots and 3 Tbsp./45 mL butter and cook for another 2 minutes. Lower the heat to medium. Add the artichokes and peas. Cook another 2 minutes. Add the wine and 6 Tbsp./90 mL butter and simmer over low heat for 5–8 minutes. Season with salt and pepper to taste.

Serve the stew in a casserole dish, sprinkled with parsley.

Serves 4.

^ Suggested Wine

Medium-bodied red

Italy
Lungarotti Rubesco

Australia
Lindeman's Cabernet Sauvignon "Bin 45"

France
Jaffelin Auxey-Duresses

> Suggested Wine

Full-bodied red

Italy
Antinori Solaia

France
Château Clarke

United States (California)
Rutherford Vintners Cabernet Sauvignon Reserve

Cosciotto d'agnello
Roasted Leg of Lamb

6   lb./2.5 kg leg of lamb
4   whole cloves garlic, peeled
1   tsp./5 mL coarsely chopped
    fresh rosemary
1   tsp./5 mL coarsely chopped
    fresh sage
2   Tbsp./30 mL Dijon mustard
1   Tbsp./15 mL olive oil
1   tsp./5 mL salt
1   tsp./5 mL cracked black
    peppercorns
1   onion, skin on, halved
2   stalks celery, cut into 2 inch/5 cm
    lengths
2   medium carrots, cut into 2 inch/
    5 cm lengths

Preheat oven to 450°F/230°C.

Trim any excess fat from the lamb. Cut 1 inch/2.5 cm slits in the lamb and stud with the cloves of garlic.

In a small bowl, mix the herbs, mustard, oil and seasonings to make a paste. Coat the lamb evenly with this mixture, using a rubber spatula or the palm of your hand. Place the lamb in a large roasting pan.

Place the onion, celery and carrots around the lamb in the roasting pan. Roast in the preheated oven for 60–70 minutes for rare lamb (longer if you prefer your meat well done).

Remove from the oven, discard vegetables and let stand 15 minutes before slicing. Spoon the juice from the roasting pan over the lamb before serving. Serve on a large platter surrounded by roasted vegetables of your choice.

Serves 6.

Filettini di agnello ai funghi e prezzemolo
Mignonette of Lamb with Mushrooms and Parsley

1½ lb./750 g lamb loin, cut into
   ½ inch/1.5 cm cubes
   salt
   freshly ground black pepper

Parsley Cream Sauce
6   Tbsp./90 mL butter
1   shallot, finely diced
1   cup/250 mL fresh parsley stems,
    washed and well dried
¾   cup/175 mL whipping cream
    salt
    freshly ground black pepper

½   lb./250 g fresh mushrooms (oyster,
    stone or champignon), trimmed
    and washed
6   Tbsp./90 mL olive oil
1   clove garlic, minced
    salt
    freshly ground black pepper

Season the lamb cubes with salt and pepper and set aside.

To make the sauce, melt the butter over medium heat in a medium-sized skillet. Add the shallot. When the butter starts to foam, add the parsley stems, carefully separating them with a fork. Cook for approximately 2 minutes, then add the cream and let it bubble for approximately 30 seconds. Season with salt and pepper to taste. Set aside and keep warm.

To prepare the mushrooms, chop coarsely and put in a medium-sized skillet with 2 Tbsp./30 mL of the olive oil. Brown the mushrooms over high heat for approximately 3 minutes, then add the garlic and season with salt and pepper to taste. Continue to cook over high heat, stirring carefully, until the garlic is golden brown. Remove from the heat and keep warm.

In another medium-sized skillet, heat the remaining 4 Tbsp./60 mL of olive oil over high heat. When the oil is almost smoking, cook the lamb for approximately 6–8 minutes, turning to cook on all sides. Remove from the heat.

Arrange the lamb on individual warm plates. Cover with the mushrooms and spoon the parsley cream sauce over.

Serves 4.

Suggested Wine

Medium- to full-bodied red

Italy
Antinori "Tignanello"

France
Château d'Angludet Margaux

Australia
Wynn's Coonawarra Cabernet Sauvignon

Spezzatino d'agnello
Lamb Stew

3   lb./1.5 kg lamb, cut into 2 inch/
    5 cm cubes
5   cups/1.25 L cold water
2   cloves garlic, finely chopped
    pinch fresh rosemary
6   baby carrots, diced large
6   baby turnips, diced large
1   leek, white part only, diced large
    salt
    freshly ground black pepper
1   Tbsp./15 mL finely chopped
    fresh parsley

Put the lamb in a large pot and cover with cold water. Add the garlic and rosemary and bring to a boil over high heat, then reduce the heat and simmer for 45 minutes, frequently skimming the froth off the top. Add the carrots, turnips and leek to the lamb and simmer over low heat for another 20 minutes, until the vegetables are tender. Season with salt and pepper to taste.

Serve the lamb stew in a warm serving bowl or on warm plates. Sprinkle with the parsley.

Serves 6–8.

Suggested Wine

Medium-bodied red

Italy
Val di Sugga Rosso di Montalcino

Australia
Wolf Blass Yellow Label Cabernet-Shiraz

United States (California)
Benziger Cabernet Sauvignon Sonoma

Filetto di maiale all'aceto balsamico e rafano
Pork Fillet in Balsamic Vinegar and Horseradish Sauce

8   fillets of pork or thin chops,
     2½ oz./70 g each
2   Tbsp./30 mL butter
2   cloves garlic, peeled
¾   cup/175 mL dry white wine
½   tsp./2 mL salt
¼   tsp./1 mL freshly ground
     black pepper

¾   cup/175 mL chicken stock
     (see recipe, p. 147)
3   plum tomatoes, seeded, skinned
     and finely chopped
1   tsp./5 mL balsamic vinegar

1½   Tbsp./25 mL prepared horseradish

Sauté the pork fillets in butter with garlic in a medium-sized skillet over medium heat. As soon as the pork is nicely browned on both sides, remove the garlic. Pour in the wine and cook gently until it reduces to about 2 Tbsp./30 mL. Season with salt and pepper, then remove the fillets from the pan.

Add the chicken stock to the pan juices along with the tomatoes and continue to cook until the sauce thickens. Add the balsamic vinegar and cook for 1–2 minutes.

Arrange the pork fillets on a serving dish or on individual plates. Pour the sauce on top and sprinkle with horseradish.

Serves 4.

Suggested Wine

Full-bodied white to medium-bodied red

Italy
Antinori Santa Christina (red)

United States (California)
Vendange Sonoma Chardonnay (white)

Canada (British Columbia)
Gray Monk Ehrenfelser (white)

Maiale arrostito
Pork Roast in Herbs and White Wine

*4–5 lb./1.75–2.5 kg pork butt roast,
  deboned and tied*
*1   tsp./5 mL finely chopped
  fresh rosemary*
*2   tsp./10 mL finely chopped
  fresh sage
  salt
  freshly ground black pepper*
3   cloves garlic, cut into slivers
2   cups/500 mL dry white wine
2   potatoes, peeled and diced large
1   large onion, diced large
2   medium carrots, diced large
2   stalks celery, diced large

Sauce
2   Tbsp./30 mL dry white wine
*1   cup/250 mL whipping cream
  salt
  freshly ground black pepper*

*2   tsp./10 mL finely chopped
  fresh parsley*

Preheat the oven to 400°F/200°C.

Rub the pork with the rosemary and sage. Season with salt and pepper. Using the point of a sharp knife, make incisions in the surface of the pork and insert the slivers of garlic into the incisions.

Put the pork in a roasting pan and pour the wine into the bottom of the pan. Roast meat in the preheated oven for 20 minutes, then reduce the heat to 325°F/160°C, add the vegetables and cook for 2½–3 hours (35 minutes per pound/70 minutes per kilogram), basting the pork with the pan juices approximately every 10 minutes. To test for doneness, pierce the meat with a fork. If the juices run clear yellow with no traces of pink, the roast is done.

Remove the pork from the roasting pan and keep warm. Strain the vegetables and pan juices into a small pot through a sieve, mashing the vegetables to get all their juices. Discard the vegetables and put the pot over medium heat.

To make the sauce, add the wine to the juices and stir until well blended. Add the cream, stir until well blended and cook over medium heat until the sauce thickens slightly. Season with salt and pepper to taste.

Put the pork on a warm serving platter and carve into slices. Serve on warm plates, coated with the sauce and sprinkled with parsley.

Serves 6–8.

Suggested Wine

Medium- to full-bodied white

Italy
Batasiolo Chardonnay delle Langhe

France
Guigal Côtes-du-Rhône Blanc

Canada (Ontario)
Hillebrand Estates Chardonnay

Meat, Fowl, Game

Arrosto di bue
Roast Beef

3–4 lb./1.5–2 kg boned rib roast
 of beef
 salt
 freshly ground black pepper
2 cloves garlic, halved
1 Tbsp./15 mL olive oil
2 Tbsp./30 mL butter
1 whole carrot
1 onion, halved
1 stalk celery
1 cup/250 mL dry red wine

Preheat the oven to 500°F/260°C.

Sprinkle the beef generously with salt and pepper. With a sharp knife, cut slits in the meat and insert the garlic halves. Rub the meat with the oil and butter and place in a roasting pan. Sear in the preheated oven for about 10 minutes, until the meat starts to colour. Reduce the heat to 350°F/180°C. Add the vegetables and wine and continue to cook— 20 minutes per pound for rare beef, longer if you prefer your meat well done. During the cooking period, baste the roast with the pan juices.

When the meat is done to your liking, allow it to rest for 10–15 minutes in a warm place.

Roast beef is best served with its own juice when carved at the table. Or, deglaze the pan with 1 cup/ 250 mL beef stock (see recipe, p. 146). Bring the juices and stock to a boil for 1–2 minutes, until thickened. Pour through a sieve into a sauce boat.

Serves 6.

Bistecca alla fiorentina
Marinated Porterhouse Steak

2 lb./1 kg Porterhouse steak
 salt
 freshly ground black pepper

Marinade
2 Tbsp./30 mL dry red wine
 juice of ½ lemon
2 cloves garlic, finely chopped
1 cup/250 mL olive oil
 olive oil, for frying
½ lemon, cut into wedges

Season the steak heavily with salt and pepper. Use more seasoning than you normally would.

To prepare the marinade, mix the wine, lemon juice and garlic in a bowl. Slowly add the oil in a steady stream, whisking constantly in the same direction, until well blended.

Put the steak in a shallow glass or ceramic dish just large enough to hold it and pour the marinade over. Refrigerate for at least 12 hours, turning the steak occasionally.

This recipe is best when the meat is cooked on a barbecue, but it can be panfried. To do so, coat the bottom of a heavy skillet with 2 Tbsp./30 mL olive oil. Sear the steak on both sides over high heat, then lower the heat to medium and sauté until done as desired.

Carve the meat from the bone and cut the steak in two. Serve on warm plates, garnished with lemon wedges.

Serves 2.

< Suggested Wine

Full-bodied red

Italy
Monsanto "Il Poggio" Chianti Classico Riserva

United States (Washington)
Hogue Cellars Merlot

United States (California)
Ridge Vineyards Zinfandel

^ Suggested Wine

Medium- to full-bodied red

Italy
Selvapiana Chianti Rufina Riserva

France
Château Haut-Bages-Averous

Chile
Don Melchor Concha y Toro Cabernet Sauvignon

Stufato di coda di bue e gremolata
Stewed Oxtails with Tomato Relish

2	lb./1 kg oxtails, cut into 1 inch/2.5 cm thick rounds
	salt
	freshly ground black pepper
	flour (to coat)
3	Tbsp./45 mL olive oil
2	medium carrots, peeled and cut into 1 inch/2.5 cm thick slices
3	stalks celery, split lengthwise and cut into 1 inch/2.5 cm pieces
1	medium-sized yellow onion, peeled and cut into 1 inch/2.5 cm pieces
1	medium-sized leek, white part only, washed, trimmed and cut into 1 inch/2.5 cm thick pieces
4	medium-sized fresh tomatoes, chopped
1	cup/250 mL dry red wine
1	cup/250 mL chicken stock (see recipe, p. 147)

2	unpeeled cloves garlic, mashed
1	sprig fresh parsley
1	sprig fresh thyme
2	bay leaves
	pinch fresh tarragon
3	Tbsp./45 mL balsamic vinegar
	salt
	freshly ground black pepper

Tomato Relish

½	cup/125 mL tomato concassé (see recipe, p. 145)
1	Tbsp./15 mL minced shallot
1	tsp./5 mL minced garlic
1	Tbsp./15 mL olive oil
1	Tbsp./15 mL balsamic vinegar
1	Tbsp./15 mL chopped fresh basil
1	Tbsp./15 mL finely chopped fresh chives

Preheat the oven to 400°F/200°C.

Season the oxtail rounds with salt and pepper. Lightly flour the rounds, shaking off any excess.

In a heavy-bottomed, ovenproof pot, heat the olive oil over medium heat. When the oil is hot, add the oxtail rounds and brown on all sides for approximately 5–8 minutes. Remove the oxtails from the pot and set aside.

Take out all but 3 Tbsp./45 mL of the fat in the pot and add the carrots, celery, onion and leek. Sauté the vegetables for approximately 10–15 minutes, until golden brown. Add the oxtails, tomatoes, wine, chicken stock, garlic, herbs and vinegar. Season with salt and pepper to taste. Bring to a simmer, cover and place in the preheated oven. Cook until the oxtails are tender, about 2 hours. Skim the fat from the surface of the pot.

To make the tomato relish, just before serving mix all of the ingredients in a medium bowl. Serve the oxtail rounds on warm plates, sprinkled with the relish.

Serves 4.

Suggested Wine

Medium-bodied red

Italy
Masi Campofiorin

New Zealand
Longridge Cabernet Sauvignon

Animelle con asparagi
Sweetbreads with Asparagus in a Vinaigrette Dressing

12 oz./350 g calf sweetbreads, cleaned
1   lb./500 g fresh asparagus
    salt
    freshly ground black pepper

Vinaigrette
1   medium shallot, finely chopped
4   Tbsp./60 mL balsamic vinegar
½   tsp./2 mL chopped fresh oregano
2   Tbsp./30 mL olive oil

¼   cup/50 mL flour
2   Tbsp./30 mL butter
    salt
    freshly ground black pepper

Soak the sweetbreads in cold water for 1–2 hours. Drain, then place in a saucepan with fresh water, cover and bring to a boil. Drain, cover with salted water and bring to a boil again. Rinse in cold water and drain. Cut into ½ inch/1.5 cm slices and season with salt and pepper to taste.

Trim and clean the asparagus and cut into 4 inch/10 cm lengths. Boil in salted water for approximately 8 minutes. Drain, leaving just a bit of water. Set aside.

To make the vinaigrette, in a small saucepan over low heat, cook the shallot in the vinegar for about 2 minutes. Remove the shallot and add the oregano and olive oil. Set aside.

Lightly flour the sweetbreads, shaking off the excess. In a large skillet, sauté the sweetbreads in the butter over medium heat for 2–3 minutes. Brown on both sides, then turn off the heat and keep warm in the skillet. Drain the asparagus and arrange on four warm plates. Set the sweetbreads on top of the asparagus and coat with the vinaigrette. Season with salt and pepper to taste.

Serves 4.

> ## Suggested Wine

Dry, fruity, light-bodied red

Italy
Boscaini Bardolino Classico Superiore

France
Château St. Nabor Côtes du Rhône

Spain
Bodegas Martinez Bujanda Conde de Valdemar Crianza

Pollo con peperoncini forti
Braised Chili Chicken

2½ lb./1.25 kg young chicken
    salt
    freshly ground black pepper
2   Tbsp./30 mL olive oil
2   Tbsp./30 mL butter
1   medium onion, chopped
4   cloves garlic, minced
2   sprigs fresh rosemary, chopped
6   fresh sage leaves, chopped
3   sprigs fresh thyme, chopped
1   small red chili pepper, chopped
½   cup/125 mL dry white wine
    juice of ½ lemon
1   cup/250 mL fresh tomatoes, seeded and diced

Preheat the oven to 350°F/180°C.

Cut the chicken into 10 small pieces. Season with salt and pepper. Heat the oil and butter in a medium-sized ovenproof skillet over medium heat and brown the chicken pieces, approximately 5–8 minutes. Add the onion, garlic, herbs and chili pepper to the pan. Sauté for 2 more minutes.

Add the wine, lemon juice and tomatoes to the skillet. Place in the preheated oven and bake for 25 minutes. Remove the chicken from the skillet to warm plates and serve.

Serves 2.

Involtini di tacchino
Turkey with Belgian Endive Pizzaiola

2	fillets of turkey, 6–8 oz./ 175–200 g each		2	leaves of medium Belgian endive
	salt		1	Tbsp./15 mL flour
	freshly ground black pepper		¼	cup/50 mL olive oil or vegetable oil
1	tsp./5 mL finely chopped shallot or garlic		2	Tbsp./30 mL dry white wine
¼	tsp./1 mL finely chopped fresh oregano		1	cup/250 mL tomato sauce (see recipe, p. 149)
1	cup/250 mL chicken stock (see recipe, p. 147)		1	oz./25 g mozzarella cheese, sliced into 2 pieces
2	Tbsp./30 mL dry white wine or water		2	tsp./10 mL finely chopped fresh parsley

Preheat the oven to 400°F/200°C.

Pound the turkey fillets lightly to flatten them. Season with salt and pepper to taste. Season one side of each turkey fillet with the shallot (or garlic) and oregano.

In a saucepan, bring the chicken stock and wine (or water) to a boil over high heat. Add the endive and boil for 1 minute, then drain. Discard the cooking liquid.

Roll up each seasoned turkey fillet in an endive leaf and secure with a wooden cocktail stick. Lightly dust the rolled fillets with flour. Sauté the fillets on both sides in hot oil in an ovenproof skillet until lightly browned. Discard any excess oil from the skillet and remove the cocktail sticks.

In a medium bowl, combine the wine and the tomato sauce and stir until well blended. Pour the sauce over the fillets. Put a slice of mozzarella cheese on top of each fillet. Place the skillet in the preheated oven and bake for 12–15 minutes.

Serve the turkey fillets on a warm serving platter or on warm plates, garnished with parsley.

Serves 2.

Suggested Wine

Medium-bodied white to light-bodied red

Italy
Zonin Pinot Nero "Il Bosco" (red)

Australia
Lindeman's Sauvignon Blanc "Bin 95" (white)

Bulgaria
Haskovo Sophia Merlot Reserve (red)

Meat, Fowl, Game

Petto di tacchino al sedano, rapa e zucca
Roasted Turkey Breast with Celery Root and Squash

½ turkey breast, with bone, about 2 lb./1 kg
1½ tsp./7 mL dried sage
    salt
    freshly ground black pepper
2 Tbsp./30 mL olive oil
½ cup/125 mL chopped onion
4 sprigs fresh thyme
1 cup/250 mL chicken stock (see recipe, p. 147)
3 Tbsp./45 mL butter

½ lb./250 g butternut squash, peeled and cut into ¼ inch/5 mm sticks
1 medium celery root, peeled and cut into ¼ inch/5 mm thick pieces
1 Tbsp./15 ml brown sugar
1 Tbsp./15 mL fresh sage
    salt
    freshly ground black pepper
    juice from ½ lemon
1 Tbsp./15 mL finely chopped fresh parsley

Preheat the oven to 400°F/200°C.

Remove the breast meat from the bone in one piece, keeping on as much of the skin as possible. Chop the bones into 2 inch/5 cm pieces and set aside. Rub the breast with dried sage and season with salt and pepper.

Heat the oil in a medium-sized heavy-bottomed skillet over medium heat. Add the breast, skin side down. Cook until the skin is well browned, approximately 5–8 minutes. Remove the breast from the skillet and set aside.

Add the chopped bones and the onion to the skillet and cook until the onions are golden brown, approximately 5–6 minutes. Add the thyme sprigs and chicken stock, lower the heat and simmer for 5–8 minutes. Add the turkey breast. Place in the preheated oven for approximately 20–25 minutes.

While the turkey is roasting, heat the butter in a large sauté pan over medium heat. Add the squash, celery root, brown sugar and sage. Season with salt and pepper to taste and cook over medium heat for approximately 10–12 minutes, stirring frequently, until the vegetables are tender and lightly browned. Remove from the heat and keep warm.

When the turkey is done, remove from the oven, cover and set aside. Strain the juices from the skillet into a small saucepan and set over high heat to reduce the liquid (approximately 5–8 minutes), skimming if necessary. Adjust the seasoning and drizzle with the lemon juice.

Place the turkey breast on warm dishes, spoon the sauce over and garnish with the vegetables. Sprinkle with fresh parsley.

Serves 4.

Suggested Wine
Rich, full-bodied white or rosé

Italy
Antinori Borro della Sala (white)

France
Domaine St. Hilaire Côtes de Provence (rosé)

United States (California)
Bonny Doon Vin Gris de Cigare (rosé)

Meat, Fowl, Game

Pollo cremato con piselli
Creamed Chicken with Spring Peas

1	whole stewing chicken, washed (liver removed)		**Creamed Pea Sauce**
		3	Tbsp./45 mL butter
1	medium carrot, peeled and sliced	2	medium leeks, white part only, thinly sliced
2	celery stalks, sliced	2	Tbsp./30 mL flour
1	small leek, sliced	2	cups/500 mL chicken stock
1	bay leaf		salt
2	small onions, peeled and sliced		freshly ground black pepper
3	parsley stems	1	cup/250 mL whipping cream
3	sprigs fresh thyme	1	cup/250 mL fresh or frozen green peas
12	cups/3 L cold water		
		1	Tbsp./15 mL finely chopped fresh parsley

In a stock pot, combine all the ingredients except the chicken and sauce and bring to a boil over high heat. Reduce to a simmer, then add the whole chicken. Simmer uncovered for approximately 30 minutes. Remove the chicken from the pot. When it is cool enough to handle, discard the skin, remove the meat from the bones, cut it into small slices and refrigerate. Return the bones and remaining scraps of meat to the stock pot and continue to simmer uncovered for approximately 1 hour. Remove from the heat, strain the stock through a sieve lined with a fine linen or muslin cloth and cool in a bowl over ice water. Skim the fat from the stock.

Note: Leftover stock can be frozen in ice cube trays for up to several weeks or can be used for other recipes.

To make the cream sauce, melt the butter in a large saucepan over medium heat. Add the leeks, cover and cook for approximately 5 minutes, stirring occasionally. Reduce the heat and stir in the flour. Add 2 cups/500 mL of the chicken stock to the pan, season with salt and pepper to taste and cook for approximately 10–12 minutes, stirring occasionally. Add the cream to the pan and continue cooking for 5 more minutes until the sauce starts to thicken. Add the peas and the chicken slices and simmer for approximately 2 minutes. Arrange the chicken slices on warm plates and spoon the sauce over. Sprinkle with fresh parsley. Best served with steamed rice.

Serves 4.

> Braised Chili Chicken, *page 111*

Fricassea di pollo ai cetrioli
Stewed Chicken and Cucumber

2½ lb./1.25 kg chicken, whole
　　salt
　　freshly ground black pepper
½　carrot, diced
½　medium onion, diced
½　celery stalk, diced
½　small leek, diced
1　clove garlic, diced
4　sprigs fresh thyme
6　Tbsp./90 mL butter

2　medium cucumbers, peeled and
　　diced in ½ inch/1.5 cm cubes
½　cup/125 mL port wine
⅓　cup/75 mL whipping cream
4　Tbsp./60 mL tomato concassé
　　(see recipe, p. 145)
　　salt
　　freshly ground black pepper
2　Tbsp./30 mL finely chopped
　　fresh parsley

Preheat the oven to 400°F/200°C.

Cut the chicken into 6 pieces; cut off the wing tips at the joints and discard, remove the chicken meat from the carcass and set aside. Break the carcass into small pieces. (You can have your butcher do this for you.) *Make sure that the skin is left on the chicken.* Season the chicken pieces with salt and pepper.

In a large heavy-bottomed skillet over medium heat, sauté the carrot, onion, celery, leek, garlic and thyme in 4 Tbsp./60 mL of the butter for approximately 3 minutes, then add the carcass of the chicken and let it cook for 5 more minutes. Add the chicken meat to the skillet, skin side up, and cook for 5 minutes over medium heat. Turn the chicken pieces over, place the skillet in the preheated oven and bake for approximately 8 minutes. Remove the chicken meat only from the skillet and keep warm. After approximately 5 minutes, remove the skillet from the oven and set aside.

Blanch the cucumber cubes in a pot of boiling water for 20 seconds, drain, then set aside.

Reheat the chicken carcass in the skillet for about 5 minutes, then add the wine. Let simmer for approximately 5 minutes. Drain the juices from the carcass into a medium-sized saucepan, bring to a boil and add the cream. Turn the heat to low and carefully stir until the sauce starts to thicken. Stir in the cucumber cubes, then add the tomato concassé and whisk in the remaining 2 Tbsp./30 mL of butter. Season with salt and pepper to taste.

Serve the chicken pieces on warm serving plates garnished with the cucumber and tomato sauce. Sprinkle with fresh parsley.

Serves 6.

Suggested Wine

Medium-bodied red

Italy
Brolio Barone Ricasoli Chianti Classico
Vietti Nebbiolo delle Langhe "Perbacco"

France
Fortant de France Syrah

Australia
Rosemount Shiraz-Cabernet

Bianco di pollo aglio e rosmarino
Grilled Chicken Breasts and Garlic-Rosemary Butter

Marinade

5	Tbsp./75 mL white wine
1/4	cup/50 mL brandy
2	Tbsp./30 mL apple cider vinegar
1	tsp./5 mL fresh black pepper, cracked
1	Tbsp./15 mL coarsely chopped garlic
1/4	cup/50 mL olive oil

Garlic-Rosemary Butter

6	garlic bulbs, trimmed
1/2	cup/125 mL chopped fresh rosemary
1½	cups/375 mL soft butter

1	Tbsp./15 mL salt
1	tsp./5 mL freshly ground black pepper
	juice of 3 lemons
4	chicken breasts
2	Tbsp./30 mL Dijon mustard
1/2	tsp./2 mL salt
3	sprigs fresh sage
3	sprigs fresh thyme
6	sprigs fresh rosemary
2	Tbsp./30 mL olive oil
	salt
	freshly ground black pepper

For the marinade, combine the wine, brandy, vinegar and pepper in a saucepan, place over high heat and bring to a boil. Keep the mixture boiling until it is reduced by half, then remove from the heat and let cool. Add the garlic and olive oil. Set aside.

To make the garlic-rosemary butter, preheat the oven to 350°F/180°C. Place the garlic bulbs in a roasting pan and roast until tender and cooked through, about 1 hour. Squeeze out the soft pulp from each clove, place in a bowl with the rosemary, butter, seasonings and lemon juice and mix well. Refrigerate for at least 2 hours before using.

Rub the chicken breasts with the mustard. Place in a baking dish and sprinkle with the salt, sage, thyme and 2 sprigs of the rosemary. Add the marinade to the chicken, cover tightly and refrigerate overnight, turning the meat several times.

Remove the chicken breasts from the dish and pat dry. Rub with the oil and season with salt and pepper to taste. Place the chicken breast, skin side down, on the grill and cook over low heat until golden brown and crisp. Baste with the garlic-rosemary butter, reserving at least 4 tsp./20 mL. Turn and cook on the other side for 10–12 minutes. Place each chicken breast on a hot dinner plate with 1 tsp./5 mL of garlic rosemary butter on top and garnish with a sprig of rosemary. Serve with baked potatoes or grilled peppers.

Serves 4.

Suggested Wine

Full-bodied white or light- to medium-bodied red

Italy
Casarsa Merlot Grave del Friuli (red)

United States (California)
Preston Fumé Blanc Cuvée de Fumé (white)
Mirassou Harvest Reserve Pinot Noir (red)

warmth and

simplicity

Coniglio in porchetta
Rabbit Stuffed with Bacon and Rosemary

1	cup/250 mL water	1	sprig fresh rosemary,
1	cup/250 mL vinegar		finely chopped
3	lb./1.5 kg rabbit, including the	4	fresh sage leaves, finely chopped
	heart and liver	1	cup/250 mL olive oil
	salt	2	oz./60 g salt pork, chopped
	freshly ground black pepper	1	cup/250 mL dry white wine
2	slices bacon, cut into squares		salt
2	cloves garlic, finely chopped		freshly ground black pepper
1	tsp./5 mL fennel seeds	2	potatoes, peeled and diced

Mix the water and vinegar. Wash the rabbit in the water and and vinegar mixture, then dry with a cloth. Season the inside with salt and pepper.

Finely chop the heart and liver and mix well with half of the bacon, garlic, fennel seeds, rosemary and sage. Adjust the seasoning. Stuff the cavity of the rabbit with this mixture, and sew, or truss with skewers, to keep the stuffing in.

Heat the oil and salt pork in a large saucepan over medium heat and gently brown the rabbit with the remaining bacon, garlic, fennel seeds, rosemary and sage for about 5–8 minutes, turning from time to time. When the rabbit is well browned, add the wine and cook for a few minutes until it is reduced. Season with salt and pepper to taste. Add the diced potatoes, cover the saucepan and cook over moderate heat for 30–40 minutes, until the rabbit is tender. Remove the rabbit, cool slightly, slice the meat and serve on a warm platter with the potatoes.

Serves 4.

Suggested Wine

Medium-bodied red

Italy
Fontanafredda Barbera d'Alba

South Africa
Simonsig Shiraz

Spain
Bodegas Monticello Viña Cumbrero Crianza

Fagiano con pesche caramellate
Roasted Pheasant with Fennel and Peaches

2½–3 lb./1–1.5 kg whole pheasant
  salt
  freshly ground black pepper
28 oz./796 mL can peach halves
  (packed in natural juice)
2 Tbsp./30 mL butter
2 Tbsp./30 mL olive oil

2 tsp./10 mL fennel seeds
5 bay leaves (fresh, if available)
2 Tbsp./30 mL grappa
2 tsp./10 mL finely chopped
  fresh parsley
  bay leaves (fresh, if available),
  for garnish

Preheat the oven to 400°F/200°C.

Have the butcher debone the pheasant, leaving 2 boneless breasts and the thighs removed from the legs. Season the breasts and thighs with salt and pepper. Set aside.

Drain the peaches, reserving the juice. Set aside.

In a medium-sized ovenproof sauté pan over medium heat, heat the butter and oil and brown the pheasant pieces, approximately 3–4 minutes on each side. Add the fennel seeds and bay leaves, and place the pan in the preheated oven for 10–12 minutes.

Remove the pan from the oven and place over medium-high heat. Add the grappa and flame. Remove the pheasant pieces from the pan and set aside, keeping warm.

Add half of the peach juice to the pan. Reduce the sauce over medium heat for 2 minutes. Adjust the seasoning with salt and pepper.

Serve the pheasant pieces on a large platter surrounded by peach halves. Strain the sauce over the pheasant and garnish with chopped parsley and fresh bay leaves.

Serves 2.

Note: If grappa is not available, brandy can be substituted.

Suggested Wine

Full-bodied white or light red

Italy
Casarsa Merlot Grave del Friuli (red)

France
Labouré-Roi Beaune (red)

Germany
Deinhard Piesporter Riesling (white)

Meat, Fowl, Game

Coniglio arrosto
Roast Rabbit

3 lb./1.5 kg rabbit
    salt
    freshly ground black pepper
1   Tbsp./15 mL Dijon mustard
½ tsp./2 mL finely chopped
    fresh thyme
1   clove garlic, cut into slivers
2   Tbsp./30 mL olive oil
2   Tbsp./30 mL butter

Preheat the oven to 400°F/200°C.

Season the rabbit heavily with salt and pepper. Rub it with the mustard and sprinkle with the thyme. Using the point of a sharp knife, make small slits in the surface of the rabbit. Insert the slivers of garlic into the slits.

In a skillet over high heat, sear both sides of the rabbit in the hot oil and butter for a total of 2–3 minutes. Coat the bottom of a roasting pan with the oil and place the rabbit in it. Put the pan in the preheated oven and roast for 35 minutes. Remove the rabbit to a warm serving platter, carve and serve.

Serves 2.

Suggested Wine

Medium- to full-bodied white

Italy
Pio Cesare Cortese di Gavi

France
Labouré-Roi Pouilly-Fuissé

United States (Oregon)
Panther Creek Melon

Spezzatino di coniglio alla senape
Rabbit Hash in a Grainy Mustard Sauce

3   lb./1.5 kg rabbit
    salt
    freshly ground black pepper
1   Tbsp./15 mL Dijon mustard
3   Tbsp./45 mL butter
3   Tbsp./45 mL olive oil
1   medium shallot, peeled and
    chopped
½ cup/125 mL dry white wine
½ cup/125 mL beef stock
    (see recipe, p. 146)
½ cup/125 mL whipping cream
    salt
    freshly ground black pepper

Have your butcher cut the rabbit into large pieces. Rinse them under cold running water and pat dry with paper towels. Season with salt and pepper and rub well with the mustard. Set aside.

In a medium-sized, heavy-bottomed skillet, melt the butter and oil over high heat. Add rabbit pieces and cook for 5–8 minutes, until browned on all sides.

Lower the heat, add the shallot and cook for approximately 2–3 minutes, until transparent. Add the wine and cook for 2 minutes. Add the stock and cook for 2 more minutes. Add the cream and simmer until the sauce is thickened. Season with salt and pepper to taste.

Remove the rabbit to a warm serving dish. Continue cooking the sauce for 1–2 minutes until thick and velvety. Pour over the rabbit and serve on warm plates.

Serves 4.

Suggested Wine

Full-bodied white to medium-bodied red

Italy
La Stoppa Alfeo (Pinot Nero) (red)

Germany
Nahe-Winzer Pinot Gris Kabinett (white)

Chile
Villa Montes Merlot (red)

Coniglio in agrodolce
Sweet and Sour Rabbit

3½ lb./1.5 kg rabbit, cut into pieces

Marinade
1   cup/250 mL sherry vinegar
1   small onion, chopped
2   cloves garlic, chopped
1   Tbsp./15 mL finely chopped
*   fresh parsley*
1   bay leaf
*   pinch fresh thyme*
4–5 black peppercorns
*   salt*

1   onion, finely chopped
¼ cup/50 mL olive oil
*   salt*
*   freshly ground black pepper*
1   cup/250 mL chicken stock
*   (see recipe, p. 147)*
2–3 Tbsp./30–45 mL sugar
¼ cup/50 mL seedless white raisins

Clean the rabbit pieces with a damp cloth.

Put all the ingredients for the marinade in a saucepan and bring to a boil over medium heat. Remove the saucepan from the heat and let cool. Put the rabbit pieces in a bowl and pour the cooled marinade over them. After a couple of hours, remove the rabbit pieces and dry them.

In a large pan over medium heat, fry the onion in the oil until soft, then add the pieces of rabbit. Pour in the marinade and continue to cook over medium heat, uncovered, for about 20 minutes. When the liquid has evaporated, season to taste with salt and pepper. Heat the stock and add to the pan. Cover and cook for an additional 20 minutes, until the rabbit meat is tender and the sauce is fairly thick.

Dissolve the sugar in 1 Tbsp./15 mL water in a separate saucepan over low heat. As soon as it begins to brown, add the sauce from the rabbit and the raisins and simmer for a few minutes. Pour this sauce over the cooked rabbit meat and mix well before serving.

Serves 2.

Suggested Wine

Rich white or light- to medium-bodied red

Italy
Barone Cornaccia Montepulciano d'Abruzzo (red)

Spain
Torres Viña Esmeralda (white)

Australia
Lindeman's Chardonnay "Bin 65" (white)

Pernice ripiena arrostita
Partridges Stuffed with Wild Rice

2   partridges, 1 lb./500 g each
    salt
    freshly ground black pepper
¼   tsp/1 mL fresh oregano

Stuffing
1   cup/250 mL cooked wild rice
1   oz./25 g pâté de foie gras, chopped
2–3 mushrooms, sliced
2   Tbsp./30 mL finely chopped
    fresh parsley
1   small shallot, finely chopped
1   Tbsp./15 mL butter
1   Tbsp./15 mL brandy
2   Tbsp./30 mL white sauce
    (see recipe, p. 145)

Sauce
2   Tbsp./30 mL grappa
2   Tbsp./30 mL dry white wine
¼   cup/50 mL veal stock
    (see recipe, p. 148)
1   tsp./5 mL butter
    salt
    freshly ground black pepper

Preheat the oven to 350°F/180°C.

Debone the partridges, leaving in the wing and leg bones. Pat the partridges with salt and pepper and sprinkle with oregano.

To make the stuffing, mix the wild rice, pâté de foie gras, mushrooms, parsley, shallot, butter, brandy and white sauce in a bowl.

Put ½ cup/125 mL of the stuffing in each partridge and close the bird by bringing the sides together and overlapping the skin at the top, then pulling the neck skin over the seam. Secure with a wooden skewer or by weaving wooden cocktail sticks through the skin.

Put the stuffed partridges, breast side up, in a buttered baking pan and roast in the preheated oven for 20–25 minutes. Remove the partridges from the pan and keep warm.

Deglaze the baking pan with the grappa and wine. Add the veal stock to the pan and reduce by simmering over medium heat until the sauce is thick enough to coat the back of a spoon. Remove from the heat, add

the butter and stir until well blended. Season with salt and pepper to taste.

Serve the partridges on a warm serving platter or individual plates, coated with the sauce.

Serves 2.

Deboning

When serving small game birds that are to be stuffed, they are preferably cooked and served with the breast and back bones removed to make for easier eating. To remove these bones, first chill the bird for 1 hour, until the flesh is firm. Then, with a sharp boning knife or similar knife, make an incision along the back of the bird from the neck to the tail and, following close to the bone, begin to cut down, slowly working the flesh free from the carcass until the leg and wing joints have been reached. These should be separated by bending the joint back and then severing from the body, taking care not to pierce the skin. Continue until the breast and back bones have all been removed.

Suggested Wine

Medium-bodied red

Italy
Batasiolo Barbera d'Alba

France
Paul Jaboulet Côtes du Rhône "Parallèle 45"

Spain
Bodegas Ochoa Ochoa Gran Reserva

Fagiano con funghi e champagne
Pheasant with Mushroom and Champagne Sauce

2½–3 lb./1–1.5 kg pheasant
  olive oil
  salt
  freshly ground black pepper
1 head of garlic, halved

Pheasant Stock
1 tsp./5 mL olive oil
2 tsp./10 mL butter
1 small onion, diced large
1 small carrot, diced large
1 stalk celery, including leaves,
   diced large
¼ cup/50 mL dry white wine
2 cups/500 mL cold water
4 tsp./20 mL butter
1 Tbsp./15 mL flour

Mushroom and Champagne Sauce
1   tsp./5 mL butter
8   large mushroom caps, thinly sliced
1   tsp./5 mL finely chopped shallot
    or onion
⅓   cup/75 mL champagne or
    sparkling white wine
¾   cup/175 mL pheasant stock
2   Tbsp./30 mL whipping cream
1   tsp./5 mL lemon juice
¼   cup/50 mL butter
    salt
    freshly ground black pepper

2   sprigs fresh parsley

Suggested Wine
Medium-bodied white

Italy
Castello Banfi Pinot Grigio "Le Rime"

New Zealand
Villa Maria Chardonnay

United States (Oregon)
Ponzi Pinot Gris

Preheat the oven to 500°F/260°C.

Remove the giblets and neck from the cavity of the pheasant, cut off the wing tips at the joints, chop these parts and set aside. Wash the bird inside and out and brush with oil. Pat the surface with salt and pepper. Put the halved garlic in the pheasant's cavity. Set aside.

To prepare the stock, heat the olive oil and butter in a casserole dish over high heat and sauté the onion, carrot, celery, giblets, neck and wing tips for approximately 5 minutes, until the meat is browned. Put the casserole dish in the preheated oven and cook for 15 minutes. Remove from the oven.

Deglaze the casserole dish with the wine, then pour the ingredients into a saucepan. Cover them with the water and bring to a boil over high heat. Lower the heat to medium and simmer until reduced by two-thirds. Strain the stock into another saucepan through a sieve lined with a cloth (linen or muslin), then return to medium heat.

Mix the butter and flour together in a skillet on medium heat, stirring constantly to make a roux, then add the roux bit by bit to the pheasant stock. Stir until well blended and simmer over medium heat for at least 5 minutes. Set aside.

Reduce the oven heat to 425°F/220°C. Put the pheasant in a shallow roasting pan and roast for 35–40 minutes.

To prepare the sauce, sauté the mushrooms and onion in butter in a skillet over medium heat until the caps are lightly browned. Discard any excess butter. Add the champagne and simmer until the wine is reduced by half. Add ¾ cup/175 mL of the stock to the mushroom-champagne sauce and simmer until the sauce thickens. Add the cream and lemon juice and stir until well blended. Remove the sauce from the heat, add the butter and stir until well blended. Season the sauce with salt and pepper to taste.

Put the pheasant on a warm serving platter and slice. Serve on warm plates, coated with the sauce and garnished with sprigs of parsley.

Serves 2.

creating a balance

between wine and food

Anatra arrosto con cachi
Roasted Duck in Persimmon Chutney

3 lb./1.5 kg duck
   salt
   freshly ground black pepper
6 Tbsp./90 mL soft butter

2 Tbsp./30 mL butter
1 Tbsp./15 mL balsamic vinegar

Persimmon Chutney

1   cup/250 mL white vinegar
2   Tbsp./30 mL brown sugar
     juice of 2 lemons
1½   tsp./7 mL finely grated fresh
     ginger
¼   tsp./1 mL ground coriander
     pinch cayenne pepper
1   cup/250 mL diced Spanish onion
¾   cup/175 mL peeled and diced
     persimmon

Preheat the oven to 450°F/230°C.

Remove the giblets from the cavity of the duck and cut off the wing tips at the joints. (You can have your butcher do this.) Reserve the liver and heart. Wash the duck inside and out and pat the outside with salt and pepper. Cut the liver and heart into ½ inch/1.5 cm cubes, season with salt and pepper and set aside.

Rub the duck with the softened butter. Place in a shallow roasting pan and roast for approximately 40 minutes. Turn the oven off but leave the duck in for another 10–12 minutes. (This prevents the skin from burning and allows the meat to continue cooking.)

In a small saucepan, melt 2 Tbsp./30 mL butter, add the duck liver and heart and brown over medium heat. Remove from the heat and drizzle with the balsamic vinegar. Stir for a few seconds and set aside.

To make the chutney, combine the vinegar and brown sugar in a medium-sized, heavy-bottomed saucepan. Bring to a boil and cook until reduced by half. Add the remaining ingredients except the persimmon. Lower the heat and simmer very slowly for approximately 10 minutes. Remove from the heat and let cool. Fold in the diced persimmon.

Remove the duck from the oven, arrange on a warm serving platter and carve. Garnish with the diced liver and heart and serve with persimmon chutney on the side.

Serves 2.

Suggested Wine

Full-bodied red

Italy
Le Pupille Morellino di Scansano Riserva

France
Guigal Côtes-du-Rhône

Spain
Bodegas Alejandro Fernandez Pesquera

Filetto di capriolo pepato
Reindeer Steak with Pepper and Brandy Sauce

4   fillets of reindeer, 3 oz./75 g each,
    cut from the leg or loin
    salt
1   tsp./5 mL crushed black
    peppercorns
    oil for searing

Pepper and Brandy Sauce
¼   cup/50 mL brandy
⅓   cup/75 mL whipping cream
    freshly ground black pepper

2   sprigs watercress

Season the reindeer with the salt and press the crushed peppercorns into the meat so that they adhere.

Cover the bottom of a heavy cast-iron skillet with oil and sear the reindeer on high heat for 1 minute per side (longer for well-done meat). Remove the reindeer from the skillet and keep warm.

To make the sauce, deglaze the skillet with the brandy. Add the cream to the brandy and grind fresh pepper into the sauce. Reduce by simmering over medium heat for 2–3 minutes.

Serve the reindeer on a warm serving platter or warm plates, coated with the sauce and garnished with the watercress.

Serves 2.

Faraona al cartoccio
Roasted Guinea Fowl

2¾ lb./1.25 kg guinea fowl,
    cleaned, giblets reserved
1   Tbsp./15 mL butter
1   sprig fresh sage
1   clove garlic, minced
    salt
    freshly ground black pepper
3½ oz./100 g pancetta slices or bacon
1   Tbsp./15 mL olive oil

Preheat the oven to 350°F/180°C.

Wash the guinea fowl well inside and out and dry it with paper towels. Melt the butter in a small saucepan over medium heat and add the giblets, sage and garlic. Fry for a few minutes, stirring. Season well. Remove the saucepan from the heat, discard the garlic and sage and finely chop the giblets. Put the giblets back into the saucepan, stirring to allow them to absorb the cooking juices, then stuff the guinea fowl with this mixture.

Sprinkle the bird with salt and pepper, pricking the skin in a few places, then lay the pancetta over it. Lightly grease a piece of foil with the olive oil, place the bird on the oiled surface, and wrap it completely. Put the package on a baking sheet, breast side up, and roast for 1 hour.

Serve the bird wrapped in the foil so that it stays very hot. Accompany with a seasonal salad and roasted potatoes.

Serves 4.

< Suggested Wine

Full-bodied, rich red

Italy
Renato Ratti Barolo Marcanseco

South Africa
Neethlingshof Cabernet Sauvignon Stellenbosch

France
Paul Jaboulet Gigondas

^ Suggested Wine

Medium-bodied red

Italy
Fazi-Battaglia Rosso Cònero

Portugal
Lusitana Garrafeira

South Africa
Kleindal Pinotage

Quaglie con uva e brandy
Quail with Grape and Brandy Sauce

4–6 *quail, 2 oz./50 g each*
   salt
   freshly ground black pepper

Stuffing
¼   *cup/50 mL cubed day-old*
   white bread
1   *tsp./5 mL finely chopped onion*
1   *Tbsp./15 mL finely chopped celery*
1   *small clove garlic, finely chopped*
   pinch fresh oregano
1   *egg*

¼   *cup/50 mL vegetable oil*

Grape and Brandy Sauce
¼   *cup/50 mL brandy*
12–15 *green or purple grapes, halved,*
   seeded and skinned
¼   *cup/50 mL veal stock*
   (see recipe, p. 148)
   salt
   freshly ground black pepper

Preheat the oven to 400°F/200°C.

Debone the quail, leaving in the wing bones and leg bones (see p. 126). Lightly season the quail meat with salt and pepper.

To make the stuffing, mix the cubed bread, onion, celery, garlic, oregano and egg in a bowl.

Put 1 Tbsp./15 mL of the stuffing in the cavity of each quail and close the birds by bringing the sides together and overlapping the skin at the top. Secure by weaving wooden cocktail sticks through the skin.

Sear the stuffed quail on both sides in hot oil in an ovenproof skillet on high heat until browned. Put the skillet in the preheated oven and bake for 5–8 minutes (quail meat will be pink even when thoroughly cooked). Remove the quail from the skillet and keep warm. Discard any excess oil.

To prepare the sauce, deglaze the skillet with the brandy. Add the grapes to the brandy and sauté over medium heat for 1–2 minutes. Add the veal stock, stirring until well blended, and reduce by simmering over medium heat until the sauce is thick enough to coat the back of a spoon. Season to taste with salt and pepper.

Put the quail on a warm serving platter or on warm plates. Coat with the sauce and serve.

Serves 2.

Suggested Wine

Medium-bodied red

Italy
Bertani Valpolicella-Valpantena

France
André Lurton Château Bonnet Bordeaux

Argentina
Penaflor Trapiche Malbec Reserve

Gnocchi, Polenta, Rice

Riso alla pugliese
Rice Apulia Style

10	*fresh mussels*
10	*fresh clams*
4	*oz./115 g calamari tubes and tentacles*
3	*Tbsp./45 mL olive oil*
2	*cloves garlic, chopped*
1	*medium onion, sliced*
1	*medium potato, peeled and cubed*
1	*yellow bell pepper, sliced*
1	*leek, white part only, sliced into rings*
½	*tsp./2 mL saffron*

1½	*cups/375 mL Arborio rice*
	salt
	freshly ground black pepper
½	*cup/125 mL dry white wine*
4½	*cups/1.125 L fish stock (see recipe, p. 146)*
¼	*cup/50 mL seeded and sliced fresh tomatoes*
¼	*cup/50 mL sliced black olives*
1	*Tbsp./15 mL chopped fresh Italian parsley*

Preheat the oven to 400°F/200°C.

Wash the clams and mussels under cold running water until free of grit. Set aside.

Cut the calamari tubes into 1 inch/2.5 cm rings, leaving the tentacles whole. Set aside.

In a large casserole dish or sauté pan, heat the oil over medium heat and cook the garlic, onion, potato, pepper and leek until they become soft, approximately 5 minutes. Add the saffron and rice and sauté for another 10 minutes. Season with salt and pepper to taste.

Deglaze the pan with the wine and 2¼ cups/550 mL of the fish stock. Cook over medium heat for another 5 minutes, stirring frequently.

Add the mussels, clams and calamari to the pan, along with the remaining stock. Cover the casserole dish, place in the preheated oven and bake for 15–18 minutes, until the rice is still firm to the bite.

Remove the casserole dish from the oven and stir in the tomatoes and olives. Serve directly from the casserole or transfer to a serving platter. Garnish with chopped parsley.

Serves 6.

Suggested Wine

Crisp, medium-bodied white

Italy
Duca di Salaparuta Corvo Bianco

United States (Oregon)
Adelsheim Oregon Pinot Gris

France
*Val d'Orbieu Les Deux Rives Blanc
Corbières Blanc*

Gnocchi piemontese
Gnocchi with Meat Sauce

2½ lb./1.25 kg potatoes, washed
      and peeled
⅔   cup/150 mL flour
2   egg yolks
2   tsp./10 mL salt
¼   tsp./1 mL white pepper

1   Tbsp./15 mL unsalted butter
3   cups/750 mL meat sauce
      (see recipe, p. 148)
¼   cup/50 mL freshly grated
      Parmesan cheese

Put the potatoes in a pot of boiling salted water. Cook until tender, about 30–45 minutes. Drain and mash by putting the potatoes through a mouli or a ricer. Set aside and keep warm.

Lightly flour a clean cutting board. Make a well in the flour. Add the egg yolks and salt and pepper, then gradually add the still-warm mashed potatoes. Mix with your hands or two forks until the potatoes are well blended and a firm-textured dough is formed. Set the dough aside and clean the cutting board. Lightly flour the board again. Roll one-quarter of the dough until it forms a rope 1 inch/ 2.5 cm in diameter. Cut the dough with a knife into ½ inch/1.5 cm pieces and pinch to shape the gnocchi, placing the pieces on a lightly floured tray. Continue until all the dough is used up.

In a large pot, bring salted water to a boil over high heat and drop the gnocchi, a few at a time, into the boiling water. When the gnocchi float to the surface, they are done. (This should take approximately 3 minutes.) Remove the gnocchi from the pot with a slotted spoon. Drain and put on a warm platter.

Preheat the oven to 350°F/180°C.

Butter the bottom of a medium-sized casserole dish. Put a layer of gnocchi in the dish and cover with a layer of meat sauce. Alternate layers of gnocchi and meat sauce until the gnocchi are used up. Sprinkle the top with Parmesan cheese. Place in the preheated oven and bake for 5 minutes. Serve in the casserole dish.

Serves 4–6.

Suggested Wine

Medium-bodied red

Italy
Fontanafredda Barbera d'Alba

Hungary
Egervin Egri Bikaver

United States (Oregon)
Firesteed Pinot Noir

Gnocchi al gorgonzola
Gnocchi with Gorgonzola

1   lb./500 g potatoes, unpeeled
1   cup/250 mL flour

Sauce

2   Tbsp./30 mL butter
1   cup/250 mL Gorgonzola cheese
½   cup/125 mL whipping cream

¼   cup/50 mL coarsely grated
    Parmesan cheese
    freshly ground black pepper

Cook the potatoes in a pot of boiling salted water until tender, then drain, peel and mash.

Spread the flour on a cutting board or flat work surface. While the potatoes are still warm, combine with the flour to form a dough. Knead just until the flour is blended in. With floured hands, roll the dough into a sausage shape about ½ inch/1.5 cm in diameter. Cut into 1 inch/2.5 cm pieces. Put the pieces on a lightly floured cloth, making sure they do not touch each other.

To make the sauce, melt the butter in a medium-sized pan over medium heat. Crumble the Gorgonzola cheese, add to the butter and let melt. Add the cream and heat until it bubbles, then set aside.

In a separate pot, bring salted water to a boil. Drop the gnocchi into the water, and as soon as they float to the surface remove them with a slotted spoon. Add the gnocchi to the Gorgonzola mixture, toss and heat for a few minutes.

Serve on warm plates sprinkled with Parmesan cheese and pepper to taste.

Serves 4.

Suggested Wine

Full-bodied white to medium-bodied red

Italy
Bertani Valpolicella Valpantena (red)

Argentina
Penaflor Trapiche Oak Cask Chardonnay (white)

Australia
Henry Lindeman Shiraz-Cabernet Sauvignon (red)

Gnocchi di pane
Bread, Parmesan and Smoked Ham Gnocchi

Gnocchi

1   large loaf of Italian bread
    (1–2 days old)
2–3 cups/500–750 mL milk
1   large egg
1   Tbsp./15 mL salt
2   Tbsp./30 mL finely chopped
    fresh basil
4   oz./100 g finely chopped prosciutto
1   cup/250 mL freshly grated
    Parmesan cheese
1   cup/250 mL all-purpose flour,
    spread evenly over a sheet of foil

Sauce

4–5 Tbsp./60–75 mL unsalted butter
3   Tbsp./45 mL extra virgin olive oil
8–10 fresh sage leaves, finely shredded

    salt
½   cup/125 mL freshly grated
    Parmesan cheese

To make the gnocchi, cut the bread into 4 or 5 thick slices and remove the crust. Break the bread into pieces, place in a medium-sized bowl and cover completely with the milk. Let soak for 15 minutes.

Strain the milk and squeeze the bread dry with your hands, trying to remove as much milk as possible. Put the bread into a large bowl. Add the egg, salt, basil, prosciutto and Parmesan. Mix with your hands until all ingredients are well combined.

Take a heaping teaspoon/5 mL of the bread mixture and shape into a ball about the size of a cherry tomato. Roll the dumpling in the flour until lightly coated and place on a lightly floured platter or cookie sheet. Repeat until the mixture is used up. Refrigerate overnight, uncovered.

Bring a large pot of water to a boil. Add the gnocchi and cook uncovered over medium heat for 4–5 minutes, until the gnocchi rise to the surface of the water.

While the gnocchi are cooking, prepare the sauce. Melt the butter in a large skillet with the olive oil over medium heat. Add the sage and stir once or twice.

Remove the gnocchi with a slotted spoon, draining off the excess water against the side of the pot. Place them in the skillet. Season lightly with salt. Stir in ¼ cup/50 mL of the Parmesan and mix quickly over low heat. Serve at once with additional Parmesan.

Serves 4–5.

Suggested Wine

Medium-bodied white to
medium-bodied red

Italy
Ca'Bolani Cabernet Franc (red)

France
Yvon Mau Merlot Côtes du Gascogne (red)

United States (California)
Fetzer Vineyards Chardonnay "Bonterra"
(organic white)

Basic Polenta

9   cups/2.25 L cold water
2   Tbsp./30 mL salt
2   cups/500 mL coarsely ground
     cornmeal mixed with 1 cup/
     250 mL finely ground cornmeal

Bring the water to a boil in a large, heavy saucepan over medium heat. Add the salt and reduce the heat slightly. As soon as the water starts to simmer gently, start pouring in the cornmeal by the handful, very slowly, in a thin stream, stirring constantly with a whisk to avoid lumps. Keep the water at a steady low simmer and stir the polenta frequently. Cook for 20–25 minutes. As it cooks, the polenta will thicken considerably and will bubble and spit at you. Keep stirring, crushing the lumps that may form against the side of the pan. The polenta is done when it comes away effortlessly from the side of the pan.

If you are planning to serve the polenta soft, spoon it directly out of the pot into serving dishes.

If you want to serve it firm, pour the polenta onto a large wooden board, shaping it with a wet spatula into a 2 inch/5 cm thick round; or spread it on a baking sheet. Let the polenta settle for a few minutes, then cut into slices and serve it with your favourite sauce.

Serves 8.

Crostini di polenta fritta con funghi selvatici
Fried Polenta with Wild Mushrooms

½   basic polenta recipe
     vegetable oil for frying
2   oz./60 g dried porcini mushrooms,
     soaked in 2 cups/500 mL of water
     for about 20 minutes
3   Tbsp./45 mL olive oil
1   Tbsp./15 mL unsalted butter
¼   lb./125 g portobella mushrooms,
     wiped clean, stemmed and sliced
¼   lb./125 g champignon mushrooms,
     wiped clean, stemmed and sliced
2   cloves garlic, finely minced
2   Tbsp./30 mL finely chopped
     fresh parsley
     salt
     freshly ground black pepper

Prepare the polenta several hours ahead so that it will become firm. Pour it onto a platter or baking sheet and spread it uniformly approximately ½ inch/1.5 cm thick. When you are ready to fry the polenta, cut it into 8 slices.

Heat 1 inch/2.5 cm of vegetable oil in a medium-sized nonstick skillet over medium heat. When the oil is hot, fry the slices of polenta two at a time until they are lightly golden on each side, about 3–4 minutes in total. Remove the slices with a slotted spoon and drain on paper towels. Keep the polenta warm in a low oven while preparing the mushrooms.

Strain the porcini and rinse them well under cold running water several times to remove any sandy deposits. Chop the porcini into small pieces. Heat the oil and butter in a large skillet over medium heat. When the butter begins to foam, raise the heat to high and add the porcini, portobella and champignon mushrooms, making sure not to crowd the skillet or they will not brown properly. Cook and stir until they are lightly golden, about 2–3 minutes. Add the garlic and parsley and cook briefly. Season with salt and pepper to taste.

Place the polenta on individual serving plates, top with the mushrooms and serve at once.

Serves 4.

Suggested Wine

Medium-bodied red

Italy
Selvapiana Chianti Rufina

United States (California)
Pedroncelli Zinfandel

France
Paul Jaboulet Côtes du Ventoux

Spiedino di polenta e cervo
Polenta and Venison Kebabs

3 cups/750 mL water	**Sauce**
1 cup/250 mL polenta	½ cup/125 mL port wine
1½ lb./750 g fillets of venison,	2 Tbsp./30 mL veal stock
at room temperature	(see recipe, p. 148)
salt	6 sprigs rosemary
freshly ground black pepper	1 Tbsp./15 mL butter, chilled
2 Tbsp./30 mL olive oil	1 Tbsp./15 mL fresh chives

Preheat the oven to 350°F/180°C.

In a heavy medium-sized pot, bring the water to a boil, then slowly stir in the polenta. Reduce the heat and continue cooking for 30–40 minutes, stirring constantly. (Polenta must be very thick for this recipe.) When the polenta is cooked, pour it into a square pan or onto a large plate about 1 inch/2.5 cm high. Let it cool completely.

Cut the venison fillets in 1 inch/2.5 cm cubes. Season them with salt and pepper to taste. Cut the polenta in slightly smaller cubes and thread on 6 kebab sticks, alternating with cubes of venison.

Add the oil to a large skillet and brown the kebabs for 3 minutes on high heat, turning often. When brown, place them on a baking sheet and bake in the preheated oven for 10 minutes.

Deglaze the skillet with the wine and veal stock, stirring until blended. Add 4 rosemary sprigs and the chilled butter, a small amount at a time. Whisk carefully until the sauce is thick.

Serve the kebabs on a warm plate coated with the sauce. Garnish with the remaining rosemary sprigs and sprinkle with the chives.

Serves 6.

Suggested Wine

Medium- to full-bodied red

Italy
Fattoria Il Poggiolo Carmignano Riserva

France
Jadot Gevrey-Chambertin, Premier Cru

United States (California)
Clos du Bois Merlot

Gnocchi di zucca con mozzarella affumicata
Pumpkin Gnocchi with Smoked Mozzarella

Gnocchi
1 small pumpkin, about 2 lb./1 kg, cut in half lengthwise
1 Tbsp./15 mL salt
1 large egg, beaten lightly
1½–1⅔ cups/375–400 mL unbleached all-purpose flour
5 Amaretto cookies, crumbled
½ cup/125 mL freshly grated Parmesan cheese

2 cups/500 mL unbleached all-purpose flour

Sauce
4–5 Tbsp./60–75 mL unsalted butter
4 oz./115 g smoked mozzarella cheese, diced
2 Tbsp./30 mL finely chopped fresh parsley

grated Parmesan cheese (optional)

Preheat the oven to 350°F/180°C.

Place the pumpkin halves on an ungreased baking sheet, cut sides up, and bake until tender, about 40–50 minutes.

Cool slightly, then remove the pulp with a spoon and discard the seeds. Put the pulp in a large kitchen towel and squeeze out approximately ½ cup/125 mL of the juices. (Do not squeeze out too much juice or the gnocchi will be dry.)

Place the pumpkin in a large bowl and season with the salt. Add the egg, flour, crumbled cookies and Parmesan cheese. Mix well with a spoon or your hands until thoroughly combined. Place the mixture in a lightly floured bowl, cover with a clean towel, and freeze for about 1 hour. The mixture will firm up and be much easier to shape into dumplings.

Remove the dough from the freezer. Spread the 2 cups/500 mL of flour evenly over a sheet of aluminum foil. Pinch off 1 tsp./5 mL of the mixture. Roll the dumpling in the flour until lightly coated and place on a lightly floured platter. Repeat until all the mixture is used up. Refrigerate the dumplings uncovered, up to several hours, until ready to use.

Bring a large pot of salted water to boil. Add the gnocchi and cook uncovered over high heat until the dumplings rise to the surface. Remove the gnocchi from the pot with a slotted spoon, draining off the excess water.

While the gnocchi are cooking, melt the butter in a large skillet over medium heat, add the mozzarella and parsley and stir together gently over low heat for a few seconds.

Add the gnocchi to the cheese mixture and stir gently until the cheese begins to melt and the gnocchi are well coated. Stir in a few tablespoons/mL of the reserved gnocchi cooking water, if the sauce seems too dry. Taste and adjust the seasoning. Serve hot, sprinkled with Parmesan cheese if desired.

Serves 6.

Suggested Wine

Medium-bodied white

Italy
Antinori Orvieto Classico Abbocatto

France
Ostertag Sylvaner Vieilles Vignes

United States (California)
Benziger Fumé Blanc

Gnocchi, Polenta, Rice

Sauces and Stocks

Stocks—chicken, beef, veal, fish—and vegetable broth are used in many recipes in this cookbook. Make them ahead and always have them on hand. They can be stored in your refrigerator in a tightly covered container or they can be frozen.

Balsamella
White Sauce

2   Tbsp./30 mL butter
2   Tbsp./30 mL flour
1   cup/250 mL milk
½   cup/125 mL half and half cream
⅛   tsp./0.5 mL nutmeg
    salt
    white pepper

Melt the butter in a small saucepan over medium heat. Stir in the flour and simmer over low heat for approximately 3–5 minutes, whisking constantly. Add the milk and cream and simmer, whisking frequently, until the sauce thickens. Season with the nutmeg and salt and pepper to taste.

Makes 1½ cups/375 mL.

Tomato concassé

2   medium-sized fresh tomatoes

Vinaigrette
3   Tbsp./45 mL extra virgin olive oil
1   Tbsp./15 mL balsamic vinegar

Core the tomatoes. Make a small x on the bottom with a sharp knife. Blanch the tomatoes in boiling water for 10 seconds, then immediately immerse in ice water. Peel the tomatoes, cut in half and carefully squeeze each half over a bowl to remove the seeds and juice (leave the tomato pulp intact as much as possible). Cut the tomatoes into ¼ inch/5 mm cubes.

Whisk the olive oil and vinegar in a small bowl, add to the tomato cubes and toss.

Makes approximately 1 cup/250 mL.

Brodo di verdura
Vegetable Broth

1   medium leek, white part only
3   large tomatoes
1   large carrot
1   large onion
2   shallots
1   stalk celery
4   sprigs parsley
    salt
    freshly ground black pepper
1   qt./1 L water
2   cups/500 mL white wine

Dice all the vegetables and put them in a large soup pot. Add the parsley and salt and pepper to taste. Add the water and wine and cook slowly over medium heat for 2 hours. Set aside to cool, then strain through a sieve lined with a fine cheesecloth.

Makes approximately 6 cups/1.5 L.

Brodo di pesce
Fish Stock

2   lb./1 kg bones from any white
    fish (no skin)
10 cups/2.5 L cold water
1   medium onion, coarsely chopped
1   bay leaf
1   medium leek, coarsely chopped
1   stalk celery, coarsely chopped
1   sprig parsley
    salt
    freshly ground black pepper

Rinse the fish bones under cold running water for 10 minutes, then put them in a pot with the cold water. Add the onion, bay leaf, leek, celery and parsley. Simmer for 35 minutes (do not let the water boil). Remove from the heat, skim the foam from the top and let stand for approximately 20–30 minutes. Strain through a sieve lined with fine cheesecloth. Add salt and pepper to taste.

Makes approximately 6 cups/1.5 L.

Brodo di manzo
Beef Stock

2   beef knuckle bones, with some
    meat still left on
4   qt./4 L cold water
1   large onion
2   small carrots
2   stalks celery
1   small leek
1   bay leaf
    pinch fresh sage
    pinch fresh thyme
    salt
    white pepper

Ask your butcher to chop the knuckle bones into large pieces. Put them in a large soup pot with the water. Add the vegetables and bring to a boil. Then turn down the heat and skim.

Season with the bay leaf, sage and thyme. Continue to simmer over very low heat for 2 hours, skimming from time to time. Carefully strain the broth through a sieve lined with fine cheesecloth. Season with salt and pepper to taste.

Makes approximately 10 cups/2.5 L.

Brodo di pollo
Chicken Stock

2   lb./1 kg chicken bones
1   small onion, halved
1   small carrot, peeled
1   stalk celery
7   qt./7 L cold water
½   tsp./2 mL salt
½   tsp./2 mL white peppercorns
1   bay leaf
1   sprig fresh thyme, chopped

Rinse the chicken bones under cold running water and place in a large pot. Add the onion, carrot, celery and water and bring to a boil. Skim off the foam that forms on the top of the pot and season with the salt, peppercorns, bay leaf and thyme. Reduce the heat to low and simmer for 1½ hours, then strain through a sieve lined with fine cheesecloth.

Makes approximately 10 cups/2.5 L.

Salsa di carne
Meat Sauce

¼ cup/50 mL olive oil
1 large onion, chopped
1 lb./500 g lean ground beef
4 cloves garlic, chopped
6 large ripe tomatoes,
   finely chopped
2 Tbsp./30 mL tomato paste
1 cup/250 mL dry red wine
1 cup/250 mL beef stock
   (see recipe, p. 146)
2 bay leaves
   salt
   freshly ground black pepper

In a large skillet on medium heat,
sauté the onion in the oil until it is
transparent. Add the ground beef
and garlic and sauté on medium heat
for approximately 5 minutes, until
the beef is evenly browned. Add the
tomatoes to the beef.

Add the tomato paste, wine, stock,
bay leaves and salt and pepper to
taste. Stir until well blended, then
cook, uncovered, on low heat for
1 hour, stirring frequently.

Makes 6 cups/1.5 L.

Fondo di vitello
Veal Stock

1 onion, diced large
1 carrot, diced large
1 stalk celery, including top,
   diced large
2–3 fresh parsley stalks, chopped
1 leek, washed and diced large
   (optional)
1 lb./500 g veal bones

1 lb./500 g veal trimmings
½ cup/125 mL cold water
½ cup/125 mL olive oil
½ cup/125 mL flour
½ cup/125 mL dry red wine
1 bay leaf
1 bouquet garni
3 qt./3 L cold water

Preheat the oven to 400°F/200°C.

Put the onion, carrot, celery, parsley and leek in an ovenproof casserole dish or
roasting pan. Cover with the veal bones and trimmings. Add the water and place
the dish in the preheated oven. Bake for 20 minutes, until the veal bones and
trimmings are lightly browned.

In a large pot, make a roux of the oil and flour, stirring constantly over medium
heat. Add the contents of the roasting pan to the pot and stir until the ingredients
are well blended. Stir in the wine, blending well, and season with the bay leaf and
bouquet garni. Add the cold water to the pot and bring to a boil over high heat,
then reduce the heat to low and simmer for 1½–2 hours, frequently skimming the
froth and excess oil from the top. Strain the veal stock carefully through a sieve
lined with a linen or muslin cloth.

Makes 6–8 cups/1.5–2 L.

Salsa di pomodoro
Tomato Sauce

2	Tbsp./30 mL olive oil	1	bay leaf
1	Tbsp./15 mL butter	1	tsp./5 mL finely chopped
1	large onion, finely chopped		fresh oregano
1	medium carrot, finely chopped	½	tsp./2 mL finely chopped
1	stalk celery, finely chopped		fresh basil
2	28 oz./796 mL cans of peeled	1	whole clove, crushed
	Italian tomatoes, finely chopped	1	Tbsp./15 mL sugar
	(liquid reserved)	½	cup/125 mL dry red wine
2	Tbsp./30 mL tomato paste		salt
4	cloves garlic, minced		freshly ground black pepper

In a large pot, sauté the onion in 1 Tbsp./15 mL of the oil and the butter until it is transparent. Add the carrot and celery and sauté on medium heat for approximately 5 minutes.

Add the tomatoes and their liquid, tomato paste, garlic, herbs, sugar and wine. Bring to a boil on high heat, stirring frequently, then simmer on low heat, uncovered, for 1 hour. Season with salt and pepper to taste.

Strain the sauce through a fine sieve. It should be thick and rich. If the sauce is too thin after straining, continue to simmer on low heat; if too thick, add a little water.

When the sauce has reached the desired consistency, remove from the heat and add the remaining 1 Tbsp./15 mL of oil, but do not mix in.

Allow the sauce to cool, uncovered, at room temperature for at least 4 hours.

Makes approximately 6 cups/1.5 L.

Burro di gamberi
Prawn Butter

2	cloves garlic, coarsely chopped
1	medium onion, coarsely chopped
1	celery stalk, coarsely chopped
3	Tbsp./45 mL olive oil
30	prawn shells
6	Tbsp./90 mL butter
7	Tbsp./100 mL dry white wine
7	Tbsp./100 mL water
3	sprigs fresh parsley
3	sprigs fresh thyme
3	sprigs fresh rosemary

Heat the oil in a medium-sized skillet, and cook the garlic, onion and celery on medium heat until brown, about 5–8 minutes.

Put the prawn shells and butter in a blender and blend until creamy. Add to the browned vegetables and cook for approximately 10 minutes on medium heat.

Add the wine and water to the skillet, together with the parsley, thyme and rosemary sprigs. Simmer on low heat for 30 minutes, then strain and let cool.

Store in the refrigerator for at least 3 hours before using. The surface fat is the prawn butter.

Prawn butter can be stored in your refrigerator in a sealed container for approximately one week.

Desserts

I have often been accused of living *la dolce vita,* "the sweet life." But I must honestly tell you that even though my life is very satisfying, I have never really developed the *dolce* (sweet) tooth. I do, however, have the greatest admiration for pastry chefs and those who devote themselves to the creation of desserts. Dessert is an art form, satisfying to the eye in both colour and design, and its preparation allows the creator a wide range of personal expression.

When you present your finest dessert at the end of a meal, it will leave your guests with a lasting memory. Dessert serves a dual function of reawakening your palate and rounding off the meal. It will be your final gift, your concluding statement.

My preference for finishing a meal has always been fresh fruit or a fruit-related dish such as fruit tart or sherbert. In this book, I share the many favourite desserts created by friends and colleagues. Among these, Patricio Sacchetto is perhaps the person who has influenced me the most; his artistic touch and the love he shows in creating dessert masterpieces are inspirational.

Since the last taste is the one you will remember, go ahead and indulge now and then in the "sweetness of life"; but keep in mind that too much of a good thing can spoil it for you.

Chocolate Sponge Cake

6   eggs, separated
¾   cup/175 mL sugar
¾   tsp./4 mL vanilla
1   cup/250 mL cake flour, sifted
½   cup/125 mL unsweetened
    cocoa powder

Preheat the oven to 325°F/160°C. Grease and lightly flour a 10 inch/ 25 cm springform pan.

In a medium-sized bowl, beat the egg yolks, sugar and vanilla until light and fluffy. In another medium-sized bowl, beat the egg whites until stiff but not dry. Fold them carefully into the yolk mixture. Combine the flour and cocoa and fold into the egg mixture. Pour the batter into the prepared pan. Bake in the preheated oven for 40–45 minutes, or until the cake tests done. Let cool completely before slicing.

Zuccotto

10   inch/25 cm chocolate sponge cake
¼   cup/50 mL cognac or brandy
¼   cup/50 mL rum
¼   cup/50 mL kirsch
3½   cups/875 mL whipping cream
1   cup/250 mL powdered sugar
¾   cup/175 mL chopped candied fruit
2–3 dark, sweet pitted cherries

¾   cup/175 mL toasted almonds,
     ground
¾   cup/175 mL toasted hazelnuts,
     ground
3–4 oz./85–115 g semisweet chocolate,
     finely grated

     Unsweetened cocoa powder and
     powdered sugar for decoration

Cut the cake into ⅓–½ inch/7–15 mm strips to fit a 3 qt./3 L mould or bowl. Combine the cognac or brandy, rum and kirsch. Sprinkle three-quarters of the cake strips with the liqueur mixture, reserving the rest. Line the mould (or bowl) with the liqueur-sprinkled strips, trimming as needed.

Beat 1¾ cups/425 mL of the whipping cream with ½ cup/125 mL of the powdered sugar until quite firm. Fold in the candied fruit. Pour into the cake-lined mould. Position the cherries in the centre and refrigerate.

Beat the remaining 1¾ cups/425 mL whipping cream with the remaining ½ cup/125 mL powdered sugar, again until quite firm. Fold in the ground nuts and grated chocolate. Pour this mixture into the mould. Top with the remaining sponge slices, trimming to fit as needed. Refrigerate for at least 2 hours. Unmould onto a serving dish and decorate with sifted cocoa and powdered sugar.

Note: This cake is best made the night before it is to be served, allowing the alcohol and moisture from the filling to be fully absorbed into the sponge.

Makes 10 pieces.

La torta di cioccolato al rum
Rum Chocolate Cake

Cake

5	*Tbsp./75 mL butter, at room temperature*
¾	*cup/175 mL sugar*
6	*eggs, separated*
2	*cups/500 mL blanched almonds, ground*
5	*oz./140 g semisweet block chocolate, grated*
¾	*cup/175 mL all-purpose flour*
½	*cup/125 mL rum*
3	*Tbsp./45 mL Amaretto*

Frosting

⅔	*cup/150 mL whipping cream*
7	*oz./200 g semisweet chocolate, finely chopped*
½	*cup/125 mL powdered sugar*
4	*tsp./20 mL vanilla*
2	*oz./60g coarsely grated chocolate*

Preheat the oven to 375°F/190°C.

Grease and flour a 9 inch/23 cm springform pan. Using an electric mixer, cream the butter and sugar. Beat in the egg yolks one at a time. Add the almonds, 5 oz./140 g of grated chocolate, flour, rum and Amaretto, mixing at a low speed. Transfer the mixture to a large mixing bowl and set aside. In a medium-sized bowl, beat the egg whites until stiff but not dry. Stir one-quarter of the beaten egg whites into the batter. Carefully fold in the remaining egg whites.

Pour the batter into the prepared pan. Bake in the preheated oven 40–45 minutes, or until a cake tester or knife inserted in the cake comes out clean. Remove from the oven. Let cool for 10 minutes, then remove from the pan and cool on a wire rack. When completely cool, split the cake into 2 equal layers.

Frosting

In a small saucepan, heat the cream until it simmers. Remove from the heat and add the finely chopped chocolate, whisking briskly until all the chocolate is melted. Stir in the sugar and vanilla. Cool slightly.

To assemble: Place the bottom layer of the cake on a plate. Top with one-third of the frosting. Top with the remaining cake layer. Spread the rest of the frosting over the sides and top of the cake. Sprinkle the 2 oz./60 g of grated chocolate over the top and sides of the cake.

Soffiato al limone
Lemon Soufflé Cheesecake

2   8 oz./227 g packages cream
    cheese, at room temperature
1   cup/250 mL sugar
½   tsp./2 mL vanilla
2   pinches salt
4   heaping Tbsp./65–70 mL corn
    starch
8   egg yolks
1¾ cups/425 mL whipping cream
2   lemons, juiced
    zest of 4 lemons
½   cup/125 mL ricotta cheese
8   egg whites
    soft butter for greasing

Preheat the oven to 350°F/180°C.

Thoroughly grease the sides and bottoms of 12 soufflé cups.

Whip the cream cheese and sugar together in a food processor. Reduce the speed and add the vanilla, salt, cornstarch, egg yolks, cream, lemon juice and lemon zest. Fold in the ricotta. In a separate bowl, whip the egg whites until stiff and fold into the cheese mixture. Fill the soufflé cups so that the filling rises ½ inch/1.5 cm above the rims. Bake in the preheated oven for 30–35 minutes. Cool and remove from the cups and refrigerate.

Serve with freshly whipped cream.

Makes 12 servings.

Torta di mele
Quick Apple Cake

Filling
6   medium Granny Smith apples
     juice of 1 lemon
¼   cup/50 mL sugar

Cake
¼   cup/50 mL butter
½   cup/125 mL sugar
2   egg yolks
     juice of ½ lemon
     grated peel of 1 lemon

1   cup/250 mL all-purpose flour
1   tsp./5 mL baking powder
6   Tbsp./90 mL milk
3   Tbsp./45 mL dark rum
3   egg whites

Glaze
2   Tbsp./30 mL butter, melted
1   egg yolk

     powdered sugar (optional)

Preheat the oven to 375°F/190°C. Butter a 1½–2 qt./1.5–2 L baking dish.

Peel, core and quarter the apples and put them in a medium-sized bowl. Sprinkle with the lemon juice and sugar. Set aside.

Cake
Using an electric mixer, cream the butter and sugar. Beat in the egg yolks, lemon juice and grated peel. Sift together the flour and baking powder. Add to the creamed mixture along with the milk and rum. Mix until well blended. In another bowl, beat the egg whites until light and fluffy, then fold carefully into the batter.

Pour the batter into the buttered baking dish. Press the apples into the batter.

Glaze
Combine the melted butter and egg yolk. Brush or drizzle over the cake.

Bake the cake in the preheated oven for 40–50 minutes. Remove from the oven and sprinkle with powdered sugar, if desired.

Makes 12 slices.

Savoiardi
Ladyfingers

¾   cup/175 mL granulated sugar
5   eggs, separated
1¾ cups/425 mL all-purpose flour
1   tsp./5 mL salt

¼   cup/50 mL powdered sugar
¼   cup/50 mL granulated sugar
¼   tsp./1 mL grated lemon peel

Preheat the oven to 325°F/160°C.
Grease a baking sheet.

Beat the sugar and egg yolks
together until creamy. Continuing to
beat, gradually add the flour and salt.

Beat the egg whites until stiff but
not dry. Stir one-third of the beaten
egg whites into the batter until it is
soft. Fold in the remaining beaten
egg whites.

Using a piping bag with a wide,
plain tip, pipe the dough into 4
inch/10 cm strips on a greased baking sheet. Allow room for the dough
to spread.

Blend the powdered and granulated sugars and the lemon peel.
Sprinkle over the dough.

Bake for 15–20 minutes or until
golden. Cool on a wire rack.

Makes about 60 ladyfingers.

Castagnole fritte
Lemon Fritters

2   eggs
3   Tbsp./45 mL sugar
1¾ cups/425 mL all-purpose flour
¼   cup/50 mL olive oil
3   tsp./15 mL brandy
     pinch salt
1   tsp./5 mL vanilla extract
     peel of 2 lemons, grated
1   qt./1 L peanut oil, for frying
     powdered sugar

Using an electric mixer, beat the eggs
with the sugar until light and fluffy.
Add the flour, oil, brandy, salt,
vanilla and lemon peel. Mix until
well blended.

Heat the peanut oil in a large
enough saucepan for deep-frying.
Take a full teaspoon of the fritter
mixture and, using another teaspoon
to help shape it, drop the batter into
the hot oil. The fritters will puff up,
so fry only a few at a time. Drain on
paper towels and dust with powdered
sugar. Serve immediately.

Makes 16–20 fritters.

Note: Strain the oil when cool and it
can be saved and reused.

Pere cotte al moscato
Pears in White Wine

3   large Bosc pears
½   cup/125 mL sugar
⅔   cup/150 mL dry white wine
⅔   cup/150 mL water
     strip of lemon peel
3   whole cloves
1   cinammon stick

Peel the pears, cut into halves and
remove the cores. Place the pears in a
large saucepan. Add the remaining
ingredients to the pan, reserving
⅓ cup/75 mL of the wine. Simmer
over medium-low heat until the pears
are tender, about 10 minutes.
Remove the pears, using a slotted
spoon, and place them in a serving
bowl. Add the reserved wine to the
cooking liquid. Bring to a boil,
reduce the heat and simmer 5–10
minutes, until the liquid reduces
slightly. Discard the cloves and lemon
peel and pour the liquid over the
pears. Cool before serving.

Serves 6.

Crostoli di Venezia
Nun's Chatter

2½ cups/625 mL all-purpose flour
¾ cup/175 mL sugar
½ tsp./2 mL salt
¼ cup/50 mL butter, at room
  temperature
1 tsp./5 mL grated lemon peel or
  orange peel
1 tsp./5 mL vanilla extract

1 egg
2 egg yolks
¼ cup/50 mL Marsala or dry
  white wine
2 Tbsp./30 mL orange juice
  milk (if needed)
  oil for deep-frying
  powdered sugar

In a medium-sized bowl, combine the flour, sugar and salt. Beat in the butter. Add the lemon or orange peel, vanilla, egg, egg yolks, wine and orange juice. Stir in a few tablespoons of milk, if necessary. The dough should be firm enough to roll out thinly with a rolling pin.

Knead dough lightly. Roll out ⅛ inch/3 mm thick on a flat, lightly floured surface. Using a pastry wheel, cut ribbons 1½–2 inches/4–5 cm wide by 3–4 inches/ 7.5–10 cm long. Cut 2 lengthwise slits in the middle of each ribbon. Twist each ribbon carefully.

In a deep skillet, heat the oil to 375°F/190°C, or until a 1 inch/2.5 cm cube of bread turns golden brown in 50 seconds. Fry the pastry strips, a few at a time, until lightly browned.

Drain well on paper towels and roll in powdered sugar.

Makes 55–60 cookies.

Amaretti
Almond Macaroons

4 cups/1 L blanched almonds,
  finely ground
1½ cups/375 mL sugar
2 tsp./10 mL vanilla extract
2 Tbsp./30 mL Amaretto
3 egg whites

Preheat the oven to 300°F/150°C. Grease and flour a baking sheet.

In a medium-sized bowl, combine the almonds, sugar, vanilla and Amaretto. Stir in the egg whites, one at a time, to make a soft, well-blended paste.

Using a piping bag fitted with a round, plain tip, pipe 1–2 inch/ 2.5–5 cm balls of dough on a greased baking sheet. Bake in the preheated oven for 20–30 minutes, or until lightly golden.

Makes about 36 cookies.

Desserts

Panna cotta al caffè
Espresso Crème Brûlée

¾ cup/175 mL milk
2 cups/500 mL whipping cream
¾ cup/175 mL sugar
1 vanilla bean, split lengthwise

8 egg yolks
¼ cup/50 mL espresso coffee (brewed)

Preheat the oven to 350°F/180°C.

In a heavy-bottomed saucepan, heat the milk, cream, ¼ cup/50 mL of the sugar and vanilla bean over medium heat, stirring occasionally, until the mixture comes to a boil. Remove the pan from the heat and set aside.

In a medium-sized bowl, beat the egg yolks, ¼ cup/50 mL of the sugar and espresso coffee. Slowly add the heated milk mixture to the egg mixture, stirring constantly. Strain the combined mixture through a sieve.

Fill six 6 oz./170 mL coffee cups or small soufflé dishes evenly with the cream mixture. Place the cups in a baking dish and pour hot water around them until the water level reaches halfway up the outside of the cups.

Place the dish in the preheated oven and bake for 30–35 minutes, or until the mixture is firm. Remove the cups from the baking dish and and refrigerate for 2–3 hours.

Before serving, cover the top of each custard evenly with a thin layer of the remaining sugar and brown under a broiler.

Serves 6.

Suggested Wine

Rich, sweet dessert wine

Italy
Maculan Picolit

Canada (British Columbia)
*Gehringer Bros. Johannisberg Riesling
Ice Wine*

Profiterole al cioccolato
Profiteroles with Bittersweet Chocolate

Pastry
1	cup + 1 Tbsp./265 mL water
½	cup/125 mL butter
½	tsp./2 mL salt
1	Tbsp./15 mL sugar
1¼	cups/300 mL all-purpose flour

3–4 eggs, each beaten separately

Pastry Cream Filling
½	cup/125 mL sugar
1	Tbsp./15 mL cornstarch
1	Tbsp./15 mL all-purpose flour
½	tsp./2 mL vanilla extract
1	cup/250 mL milk
2	egg yolks
½	cup/125 mL whipping cream
4	tsp./20 mL Marsala (optional)

Chocolate Sauce
5	oz./140 g bittersweet chocolate
⅔	cup/150 mL sugar

Preheat the oven to 400°F/200°C.

In a medium-sized saucepan, combine the water, butter, salt and sugar. Place over low heat until the butter has melted, then bring to a rapid boil. Remove from the heat.

With a wooden spoon, beat in the flour until it has been absorbed and the dough forms a ball. Cool slightly. Add the beaten eggs, one at a time, beating well with an electric mixer after each addition. If the dough is soft enough after the third egg has been added, *do not* add the fourth egg. The dough should be shiny and fairly thick.

Butter and flour a baking sheet. Using a spoon or a piping bag, place the dough in small mounds on the sheet. Bake 10 minutes, then reduce the heat to 350°F/180°C and bake 10–15 minutes longer.

Filling
In a saucepan, blend the sugar, cornstarch, flour and vanilla with the milk. Whisk over medium heat until thick. In a small bowl, beat the egg yolks slightly and add part of the hot mixture to the yolks. Blend and return to the saucepan. Reheat gently, stirring until thickened. Allow to cool. Add Marsala if desired.

Whip the cream until quite firm. Fold it into the pastry cream.

To fill the profiteroles, make a small incision in the base of each with a knife. Using a piping bag with a small plain tip, fill each profiterole with the cream filling.

Sauce
Melt the chocolate over hot, not boiling, water with the sugar. Dip each profiterole in the chocolate mixture. Arrange on a platter in a pyramid, then pour the remaining chocolate sauce over the top.

Makes 48 profiteroles.

Crema rovesciata all'arancio
Upside-Down Orange Cream

½ cup/125 mL sugar
6 Tbsp./90 mL cold water
2 medium-sized oranges, peeled
   and white part removed
2 cups/500 mL milk
3 Tbsp./45 mL sugar

½ vanilla bean
3 eggs
3 egg yolks
3 Tbsp./45 mL sugar
   peel of 1 orange, grated

Preheat the oven to 350°F/180°C.

In a small saucepan, combine the sugar and 3 Tbsp./45 mL of the water. Melt over medium heat until the sugar turns golden brown. Then add the remaining 3 Tbsp./45 mL cold water and swirl carefully to stop the sugar from cooking. Remove from the heat. Pour into a round mould just big enough to contain all the ingredients, about 1 qt./1 L.

Thinly slice the oranges about ⅛ inch/3 mm thick. Arrange the slices close together over the sugar in the mould. Set aside.

In a medium-sized pan, combine the milk, sugar and vanilla bean and bring to a boil. Remove from the heat.

In a medium-sized bowl, combine the eggs, egg yolks, sugar and grated orange peel and whisk together vigorously. Remove the vanilla bean from the milk and add the sweetened milk to the egg/sugar batter. Strain this mixture through a fine strainer and then pour over the orange slices in the mould.

Place the mould in a pan of hot water that comes halfway up the sides of the mould. Bake in the preheated oven for approximately 35–40 minutes. Remove from the oven, let cool, then refrigerate for at least 2 hours.

To unmould: Insert a knife around the edge of the mould until the cream comes free from the pan. Turn the mould upside down on a serving dish.

Serves 6.

Suggested Wine

These wines have an orange-blossom fragrance.

France
Paul Jaboulet Muscat de Beaumes-de-Venise

United States (California)
Quady Essensia

Montagna innevicata
Blackcomb Mountain Special

3½ oz./100 g white chocolate,
    chopped
3½ oz./100 g dark chocolate, chopped
4   pieces of foil or wax paper, each
    6 inches/15 cm square

Tulip Biscuits
3   Tbsp./45 mL butter, at room
    temperature
3   Tbsp./45 mL sugar
3   Tbsp./45 mL flour
2   egg whites

Filling
4   scoops each of vanilla and
    chocolate ice cream
4   Tbsp./60 mL mixed berries
    (strawberries, raspberries,
    blueberries, blackberries), warmed

powdered sugar

In a double boiler over hot, not boiling, water, melt the white chocolate and dark chocolate separately. Outline a triangle shape with white chocolate on each piece of foil or wax paper, then use a pastry brush to fill in the triangles with the white chocolate. Repeat with the dark chocolate, spreading it on top of the white chocolate. The triangles will be about ⅛ inch/3 mm thick. Place the sheets in the refrigerator. Just before the chocolate becomes firm, mould each triangle into a cone so that one end is closed, the other open. Keep the foil or paper wrapped around the chocolate cones until ready to unmould.

Tulip Biscuits
Preheat the oven to 300°F/150°C.

In a medium-sized bowl, cream the butter and sugar together until doubled in bulk. Add the flour, 1 Tbsp./15 mL at a time, blending in well. Stir in the egg whites. Place 4 separate Tbsp./15 mL of this mixture on a baking sheet, making 4 large wafers, each about 8 inches/20 cm in diameter and ⅛ inch/3 mm thick. Bake in the preheated oven until the wafers are light brown, then remove from the oven and mould each one around the outside bottom of a teacup or a custard cup until the wafers are cool and become firm. Remove from the cups gently.

Filling
Place the tulip biscuits on individual serving dishes. Arrange 1 scoop of vanilla and 1 scoop of chocolate ice cream in each biscuit. Spoon the warm berries over the ice cream. Carefully remove the foil or paper from the chocolate mountains and place one behind each biscuit. Before serving, sprinkle powdered sugar over the berries and ice cream.

Serves 4.

Suggested Wine

Serve before or after the dessert.

South Africa
Neethlingshof Wiesser Riesling Noble Late Harvest (white)

United States (California)
Quady Elysium (red)

Torta di castagne
Chestnut Tart

5¼ cups/1.25 L chestnut flour
⅔ cup/150 mL vegetable oil
½ cup + 1 Tbsp./140 mL sugar
½ tsp./2 mL salt
1 cup/250 mL pine nuts
1 cup/250 mL raisins
1 cup/250 mL water
   leaves of 1 sprig rosemary

Preheat the oven to 400°F/200°C.

Lightly oil a 10 inch/25 cm spring-form pan.

In a large bowl, combine the flour, oil, sugar, salt, ¾ cup/175 mL of the pine nuts and ¾ cup/175 mL of the raisins. Add enough water to make a soft batter of pouring consistency.

Pour the mixture into an oiled pan. The paste should not be more than ¾–1 inch/2–2.5 cm thick. (If necessary, use a larger pan.) Brush the surface of the paste with oil. Sprinkle with the remaining ¼ cup/50 mL pine nuts and raisins and the rosemary.

Bake in the preheated oven for 12 minutes, then reduce the heat to 350°F/180°C and continue to bake for another 35–40 minutes.

Transfer to a serving dish.

Serves 6.

Note: Chestnut flour can be found in most natural food or gourmet food shops.

Perfetto al Grand Marnier
Parfait with Grand Marnier

6 Tbsp./100 mL cold water
½ cup/125 mL sugar
6 egg yolks
1 cup/250 mL whipping cream,
   very cold

2 Tbsp./30 mL sugar
¼ cup/50 mL Grand Marnier

In a small saucepan, bring the water to a boil, add the sugar and cook over medium heat until the sugar is completely melted. Remove from the heat and keep warm.

In a large stainless steel bowl, mix the egg yolks with the water and sugar mixture. Put this bowl in a pan half-filled with hot water and whisk the mixture carefully until it is almost doubled, approximately 7–8 minutes. Remove the bowl from the pan of water. With an electric mixer on medium setting, beat the mixture until the batter is cool, approximately 10 minutes. Set aside.

In a medium-sized bowl, whip the cream until firm but still glossy. Add the sugar and whisk until very firm, approximately 2 minutes.

Add the Grand Marnier to the egg yolk mixture, then add this mixture to the whipped cream, a bit at a time, until used up. Pour the parfait into a 4 cup/1 L mould, or into small individual moulds, and place in the freezer for 2–3 hours. When ready to serve, wet the bottom of the mould(s) with hot water to loosen the parfait and turn over onto a chilled plate or individual chilled plates.

Serves 4–5.

Spuma al cioccolato amaro
Bitter Chocolate Mousse

½ cup/125 mL unsweetened chocolate, chopped into chunks
3 Tbsp./45 mL strong coffee
2 Tbsp./30 mL powdered chocolate

6 egg whites, at room temperature
1 tsp./5 mL lemon juice
¼ cup/50 mL sugar

In a double boiler over hot (not boiling) water, melt the chocolate chunks with the coffee and powdered chocolate. Stir carefully until all the ingredients are well mixed and creamy. Remove the pan from the heat and the inner pan from the water. Set aside and keep warm.

In a large bowl, combine the egg whites and the lemon juice and whisk vigorously until the egg whites start to form stiff peaks. (You may use an electric beater.) Add the sugar all at once and continue beating until the egg whites are very glossy. Gently add 1 Tbsp./15 mL of the beaten egg whites to the chocolate mixture, then gently fold in the remaining egg whites until combined.

Chill the mousse in the refrigerator for at least 1 hour.

Note: Mousse does not keep well and should be used the day it is made.

Serves 4–6.

Photo credits

Index

Index

Index

Index